Mothering Marley

Wounds to Wisdom: A Mother's Journey

ACCEPTANCE OF OUR CIRCUMSTANCES STARTS WITH ACCEPTANCE OF OURSELVES.

Karissa Sherwood

Mothering Marley

Hardcover ISBN: 978-1-961098-91-6
Paperback ISBN: 978-1-961098-90-9
eBook ISBN: 978-1-961098-92-3
Printed in the USA.

Joan of Arc Publishing
Meridian, ID 83646
www.joapublishing.com

✨ Enjoy Exclusive Bonuses! ✨

Thank you for reading *Mothering Marley!* As a special thank you, I've created exclusive bonuses just for you.

How to Access Your Book Bonuses

Simply scan the QR code below with your phone to unlock your special resources:

Table of Contents

Preface

I was a young wife in the thick of mothering three small children when my daughter's life presented circumstances that were completely foreign to me. I felt overwhelmed, powerless, fearful, and completely alone. I didn't know anyone in my shoes. I didn't dare speak my thoughts and feelings about it out loud. It was too painful, too incriminating, and I didn't think anyone would understand. I didn't even understand what I was feeling within myself.

I stood in front of my mother one day and pleaded through agonizing streams of tears, "Do you have any journals from any of the women in our family? Anyone on either side? I need to know that someone went through something really, really hard and that they made it through!" Sadly, she said she had nothing. The tiny flame of hope I'd held onto flickered out. My broken heart shattered into a million more little pieces. I really was all alone.

It felt safer to ask for wisdom from mothers who had passed than to look to those who were still living—the living who would judge me and my child. This was the only way I knew to ask for help. I was a desperate mother. I craved the wisdom of others that I didn't have within myself.

This book is the story of my greatest battle: my struggle, strategy, and ultimate victory. I didn't find the remedy I was seeking from a journal like I had hoped I would, but I did most definitely find it. My lived experience has molded me into the wise woman I desperately sought all those years ago.

It is my hope that this book will be that journal for you. I invite you to read these pages with an open mind and heart, keeping your own journal close by. Curiosity invites introspection, introspection invites awareness, and awareness invites change. When we know better, we do better. We can't unlock the chains if we don't know they are there.

Introduction

"Making the decision to have a child—it is momentous. It is to decide forever to have your heart go walking around outside your body."

—**Elizabeth Stone**, *A Boy I Once Knew: What a Teacher Learned from her Student*

I don't think there is a work more challenging than motherhood. There is no clocking in or out. So often we are spinning our wheels, trying to catch up. Or we are buried between the covers of our sheets, drowning in the responsibilities we carry. When our child hurts, we hurt. Their pain is our pain and their joy, our joy. Quite honestly, *their* pain strums *our* pain and even deeper than that, *they* strum our pain. Motherhood uproots our deepest pain because our children are our mirrors, constantly reflecting back to us all of our unhealed parts—places within us that are asking for more love and attention. We move about life carrying hidden *and* unhidden pain, often unaware of how these wounds shape our behaviors, choices, and presence in the world.

The lessons and wisdom I share serve as a template that can be applied in many different circumstances of motherhood, not just in mothering special needs children. The pain you feel is not about your child, it is about *you*. It all starts with you. When you can change your lens you will change your world. As you integrate these concepts, you, too, will be able to transform your deepest pain into your deepest wisdom. You are a match for your mountain. I see you. I feel you. I am you.

Karissa

PART 1

THE UNRAVELING

CHAPTER 1

The Build Up

From a very young age, the thing I wanted most was to be a mother. I had an innate sense of nurturing, tenderness, and love that came so naturally to me. My mother and I were oil and water. We fought all the time. Growing up, I never felt like she really knew me. I was a highly sensitive being who just came that way. I felt so different from and misunderstood by nearly everyone. I also held a fire that constantly got me in trouble at home. Mom and I were polar opposites, but in some ways we were very similar. I often talked back, pushing buttons and limits. I was often called ***sassy, spitfire, hardheaded, or the mouth*** *that roared.* Dad was the soft place to land. He was always the go-between for my mom and me.

I always felt like a disappointment to my parents. They held strict rules and high expectations that felt impossible to meet. After a while of constantly trying and failing, I stopped trying. I felt that my parents viewed me as difficult and bad. I was seldom doing what they wanted me to do and they often told me that when they were my age, they never did or said the things I was.

Even though I often challenged my mom, I was actually afraid of her—especially when she got angry. She would yell and chase me down the hall as I made a mad dash to my bedroom. I would slam the door and quickly lock it behind me. I sat there with my back against the wall as salty tears streamed down my cheeks. I constantly vowed to myself, ***I will not do it like this!*** And I wondered, ***Why is my mom so angry?*** Nothing I did ever made her happy. She never showed me with words or physical touch that she loved me. ***Was it all because of me? Why was I not enough to make her happy? What about me was so unlovable?***

I longed for a different relationship than what I had with my mom, but it didn't feel possible. I focused my energy on dreaming of what it would be like when I had a daughter of my own. I imagined a little girl who loved pink, took dance lessons, and shared everything with me. I'd dress her up, pierce her ears, and paint her nails. We'd be best friends. I'd hold her face, look into her eyes, and tell her how much I loved her. It would be perfect! I couldn't wait.

I married at eighteen. At twenty-one, I welcomed my first child, a son we named Drey. After twelve hours of contractions and little dilation, Drey was delivered by C-section. The day I had been anxiously awaiting for years had finally come! Despite my dreams of motherhood, the reality felt overwhelming. I didn't know how to be a mom! As I held Drey, joy mixed with fear—I was responsible for this tiny life, and I doubted my ability to manage it all. Home alone with him for the first time, I considered calling my mother-in-law to come watch him just so I could shower! With time and the daily practice, I began to find my footing as a new mother.

Down the road when I became pregnant with another boy, I was excited, though a part of me wondered if I'd ever have a daughter. My second son, Crew, was born with a very different personality. Unlike easygoing Drey, Crew was fussy, busy, and curious—traits that made mothering him a new challenge! My back ached, which I attributed to carrying him around, while an unfamiliar feeling lingered in my stomach—a sensation that food didn't satisfy. When my nursing baby was eight months old, I lay down on the couch after dinner and felt a wave of nausea that built with alarming intensity. I rushed to the bathroom as my stomach churned, and the sensation of sickness overcame me. My body shook as I threw up. My eyes closed as I endured the discomfort.

I heard my husband, Josh's, concerned voice behind me. "What have you eaten today? Anything red? Jell-O, maybe?" His questions seemed strange until I opened my eyes and saw the bright red liquid around me, pooling on the tile floor. It looked like blood, and panic set in. Josh made a few calls and insisted on a trip to the hospital. I was too weak to move, and when I glimpsed myself in the mirror, I barely recognized the pale, hollow-eyed face staring back. My father-in-law arrived to help, and together they lifted my limp frame into the car's passenger seat.

At the emergency room, Josh helped me to the bathroom as another wave of nausea hit. The next thing I knew, I was waking up on a stretcher, looking into unfamiliar faces above me. I had fainted, collapsing in Josh's arms, which fast-tracked me to the front of the line. Once in a room, the doctor suspected a bleeding ulcer and recommended an endoscopy. The small ER we were at couldn't perform the procedure, so I would have to be transferred. In the meantime, I needed a nasogastric (NG) tube to drain the blood from my stomach.

The nurses began sliding the NG tube into my nostril and down my throat, only to have it come back out when it didn't go in right. We had to try again. Each attempt left me gagging and uncomfortable as the tube scraped past my throat. The nurse told me it might be in for a couple of days—*unbelievable*. I finally fell asleep but was soon awakened by the doctor asking for Josh's permission to give me a blood transfusion. Moments later, we watched as a stranger's blood trickled into my veins. My world was turning upside down.

I was airlifted to the ICU in Phoenix. The endoscopy was performed and the gastroenterologist confirmed a bleeding ulcer, which she cauterized to stop further bleeding. She also took a biopsy for testing. She told me I'd need to stay another night. My heart sank. I longed to go home, back to my family, back to my boys. Crew was still a nursing baby and suddenly had to switch to formula for the first time. I had to pump and dump all my milk during those hospital days, and I ached for the baby who couldn't understand where his mom had gone or when she'd be back.

Every time the doctor came in, my stay stretched on longer. "Waiting for results" was all they would say, giving almost no other updates. My boys couldn't visit inside because it was RSV season, but we were allowed a short outdoor visit. As I held them and breathed in the cool, fresh air, tears streamed down my face. I cherished every moment of that precious reunion. I hugged them close, made them laugh, and soaked up the sight of their sweet little faces. When it was time to part, Josh wheeled me back to my room as my family left with the boys. Watching their little round heads moving in the opposite direction pained me!

When the doctor finally arrived with updates, we received more information in a few minutes than we had all week. I had a tumor. Surgery was necessary. The doctor reassured me it was caught early, so if it was malignant, surgery alone would be enough—no chemo or radiation. My mind was spinning, barely processing his words. They had hoped to bring good news, but still didn't have the results from the biopsy. They wanted me to stay in the hospital until results were in so I could go straight into surgery if needed. I was desperate to go home, to wait for the results with my family and then schedule surgery. After some discussion, they agreed. I was so relieved; I just wanted to be home.

On Valentine's Day, we met with the general surgeon. He rolled his seat close until he was nearly eye-to-eye with me. In a calm but serious tone, he said, "Your tumor is cancerous, Karissa. We need to remove it quickly. We've scheduled the surgery for six days from now. Afterward, you'll need to stay in the hospital for a week."

Cancer? I had stomach cancer? The cascade of escalating news was so overwhelming I could hardly comprehend it, let alone determine what it meant for me and my family. I slipped into the familiar refuge of disassociation—a coping mechanism I learned long ago to protect myself from pain too big to bear.

The surgeon sketched a diagram, explaining the procedure he'd perform. He'd remove a quarter of my stomach and create a new attachment. Tears welled up in my eyes as he described it all and assured me that, despite its aggressiveness, the cancer was caught early and surgery would be my only treatment. I'd need to adapt my eating habits, something the nurses would guide me through during my weeklong hospital recovery. I told myself that if I could just get through the surgery, life would go back to normal. But things were never meant to go back to *normal.*

Josh and I talked about how we'd handle the logistics ahead of us, but we never discussed the emotional toll. He wasn't one to show feelings, and though I was a highly emotional person, I didn't know how to connect with or process my own emotions either. Vulnerability and honest communication were foreign concepts growing up and remained so at this time. The enormity of what we were facing sat on a shelf, untouched. We were already in survival mode: Josh was building a business from scratch and supporting our family, and I was a young mom caring for two little boys and managing the household. We'd been married only five years and just beginning to navigate life together. We were young and inexperienced. This was a new mountain to climb, and we had no map.

A week later, we arrived at the hospital where Josh's dad met us to see me off before surgery. One of the things I treasure most about his dad is his presence in a crisis—he really shows up. His physical presence was a comfort, reminding me that I was supported and not alone in my pain. Lying in the hospital bed, I was wheeled into the hallway. After our goodbyes, I'd go one way, and Josh and his dad would go the other. I saw the tears well up in my father-in-law's eyes; he didn't have to say a word. His eyes said it all: *Please, wake up. Please, come back. Please, be OK.*

When I finally woke up, the room was dark, a sign the surgery had taken longer than expected. Instead of a quarter, they had removed three-quarters of my stomach. As a precaution, the surgeon had taken more of the surrounding area. He later explained that my cancer was stage 1B, the "B" indicating that cancer cells had spread into the muscle layer. With blood vessels in the muscle, there was a risk of cancer cells moving to other parts of my body. "For this reason," he said, "we highly recommend chemotherapy and radiation. You're so young. We just want to be extra cautious."

My heart sank as tears spilled over. This wasn't how it was supposed to go. The surgeon handed me the contact for an oncologist and gave me six weeks to heal before starting further treatment. My mind spun with logistics and dread. The past week had been a relentless storm of shocking news, one bombshell after another, and I struggled to comprehend the gravity of it all. *How was I going to do this? How could I manage a baby and a toddler while going through treatments?* The sheer thought of finding a babysitter every day was overwhelming. Each new thought only added to the weight pressing down on me.

Six weeks later, we met with the oncologist. His recommended treatment plan included five rounds of chemotherapy—five days a week in the first week of each month—followed by six weeks of daily radiation. I broke down in tears, feeling like I was drowning in endless waves of shock and overwhelm. Just when I thought I'd found a sliver of air, another wave hit. The oncologist explained that this chemotherapy was the mildest available: I wouldn't lose all my hair, and a port wasn't necessary unless I wanted one. That brought a small relief. I asked about future children. "It is very likely that you won't be able to," he said. I burst into tears again. He suggested I consult a fertility specialist about freezing my eggs, but it would have to be done quickly. It felt like everything I wanted was slipping away. I was desperate for hope and a simpler solution. There had to be other options!

I found another oncologist closer to home. To my dismay, he recommended the exact same treatment plan, adhering to the protocol based on established studies. The feeling of helplessness grew. I pressed again about the possibility of having more children. He explained that the radiologist could make a protective cast for my reproductive area to minimize radiation scatter, but it couldn't protect my eggs against internal scatter. My menstrual cycle would likely fade until it stopped altogether, signaling the end of any chances for more children. He rejected my bid to move toward the fertility specialist path. "We don't have time," he said. "You don't have time. This cancer is very aggressive. We need to hurry." My heart sank. All I could do was hope and pray for a miracle—and I did, every single day!

Between February and September of that year I had major surgery, chemotherapy, and radiation. I had days where I couldn't lift my head off my pillow, let alone take care of two little boys. I had to quit nursing and wrap up my breasts to dry them up. I wasn't ready to quit, and little Crew wasn't ready for that either. I racked up miles on my car, driving to and from the cancer center for appointments and treatments—sometimes, every single day. Occasionally someone went with me, but most of the time, I went alone.

At barely twenty-four years old, I felt out of place in that room of recliners, surrounded by patients old enough to be my grandparents. The atmosphere at the cancer center was heavy, something I felt the instant I stepped through the door. I saw fliers for support groups, but I dismissed the idea. ***I don't need that***, I told myself, without fully understanding why. Yes, I needed support, but I associated that need with weakness, as if support was only for those who couldn't handle their circumstances on their own. I didn't talk about what I was going through. I wasn't even processing what I was going through. I was so disconnected from myself and didn't even know it. Looking back, I know I would have benefited from talking to someone who truly understood. But at the time, I thought the best approach was to put my head down and keep putting one foot in front of the other.

Josh did everything he could to make up the difference. He came home early every evening to feed and bathe the boys and put them to bed. We coordinated family and friends to watch the boys while I was at the center. When I was home, feeling sick and drained, we had occasional help as well. Still, I tried to manage as much as possible on my own. I already felt like a burden, so I didn't want to ask for anything beyond what was offered. The amount of support we needed was more than any one person or family could provide.

One day, my sister-in-law called and asked, "How are you doing, *really*, though?" Her words stopped me in my tracks, and I burst into tears. It wasn't the question itself; it was how she asked it. Her tone held an understanding that went beyond my physical needs. Her question forced me to pause and check in with my feelings in a way I hadn't before. I'd been avoiding that, thinking I didn't have the space or time for the tidal wave of emotions waiting beneath the surface. The weight of it all felt too overwhelming to even touch.

I don't really know how we got through it. Each day dragged on, and the nights felt even longer. After my fifth chemo treatment, my lips began to bubble, blister, and peel, leaving raw, exposed flesh underneath. They burned like fire, a relentless pain that stretched through each day until new skin slowly grew to cover them. I was prescribed lidocaine to numb the area, but it barely made a difference. One day, my little niece looked up at me with a confused expression and asked, "Are you sick?" It struck me: finally, what I was feeling inside was visible on the outside. Isn't that so often the case? Only when the pain we carry is written on our faces do others see it. I wish I had a picture to capture those days, but out of embarrassment for such vulnerability, I never allowed myself to be documented that way.

In September, after completing all my treatments, I went in for a series of scans and blood tests to see where things stood. I met with my radiologist alone, again facing another appointment without support. I wondered why I was so often by myself. Asking for what I needed felt foreign, almost impossible. I constantly self-abandoned, mostly because I wasn't even sure what I needed!

The radiologist began going over every organ, reporting on each one. I'll never forget his voice saying, "Kidneys: clear. Liver: clear. Lymph nodes: all clear. Stomach: clear." From that moment on, I could hear nothing but the word "clear" echoing in my mind.

I thanked him and left the cancer center. I got into my car, closed the door behind me, covered my face with my hands, and sobbed! I was finally able to let go of all the fear, worry, sadness, and grief I'd carried day after day for eight long months. For the first time, I truly appreciated every part of my body and all it had endured to carry me through this. It's hard to understand the value of health until it's gone. I remember crying the first time I was able to make myself a peanut butter and jelly sandwich. I was declared cancer-free, given a certificate of completion from my nurses, and handed a clean bill of health. This was joy!

For a long time afterward, I cherished all the small, everyday things I couldn't manage during those eight months. Life became a series of gifts. Loading up my two little boys for well visits or outings felt like a blessing. Making us all peanut butter and jelly sandwiches felt special. Spending a full day with them on my own was something I could now truly appreciate. My boys were my motivation to get out of bed every day during treatment. I knew they needed me. Part of me feels that Drey and Crew saved me.

Throughout my treatments, my cycle was light and infrequent but never stopped completely. Regarding future children, my doctors told me that five years was the true mark of being cancer-free, but they strongly advised waiting at least two. "If you make it to two," they said, "chances are you'll make it to five." Two years felt so much more manageable than five. It felt within reach. We planned to wait.

CHAPTER 2

It's a Girl

After my treatment, I diligently kept up with my scans and blood work. Results would be discussed at my next appointment unless something concerning came up—in which case, I'd receive a phone call. So, when I saw a voicemail from the cancer center nurse just days after a scan, my heart sank! I knew what this likely meant: they'd found something. Panic set in, and I frantically called Josh, my mind racing through every grim possibility. It had only been nine months since my clean bill of health—*how could something be wrong already?*

Josh paused and asked, "Could you be pregnant?"

"What?" The thought was so out of the realm of possibility that I hadn't even considered it! "I don't know! There's no way I am!"

We hadn't been trying for a baby. My cycle had been so irregular I hadn't even kept much track of it; it wasn't time to! Should I even bother with a pregnancy test? A small flicker of excitement stirred in me, quickly followed by doubt. *Why even entertain the thought?* But curiosity and possibility got the best of me, and I rushed to the store. I left there with three tests in hand!

I followed the instructions and took a deep breath as I slowly turned the test over. A rush of emotions flooded in when I saw a bright pink plus sign in the test window! It hadn't even been a year since treatment ended. Would this baby be OK? I doubted the positive test and took two more to make sure. Each result was the same as the first.

When I finally connected with the nurse, I immediately blurted, "I think I might be pregnant! But how can that be?"

"That would make sense," she said calmly, "based on what we saw on the scan." She asked me to come in for blood work to confirm.

For days, my mind swirled with thoughts veering between hopeful excitement and cautious denial. I was instructed to meet with my oncologist to discuss my new circumstances. He asked if I planned to keep this baby. The question stunned me. He must have seen the look of shock and horror on my face.

"What's more important," the oncologist asked, "baby or mama? What if your cancer comes back while you are pregnant? This is a high-risk situation for you." He recommended that we meet with a genetic specialist to understand the potential effects of conceiving so soon after cancer treatment. More weighted circumstances that left us with little control—this felt so familiar.

On the day of our appointment with the genetic specialist, Josh and I were led into a large room that had a round table surrounded by black chairs. The genetic specialist had reviewed my medical history and treatments and read studies on other women with similar backgrounds. Josh braced for the worst while I held onto a glimmer of hope. To our surprise, the specialist said there was no evidence linking genetic disorders in babies to women conceiving soon after cancer treatment. At last, I allowed myself to exhale! Relief washed over me as I realized that everything was going to be OK!

The long-awaited ultrasound day arrived. The technician completed the routine measurements and images before turning to us with a smile. "Do you want to know the sex of the baby?" he asked.

Josh and I eagerly replied, "Yes!" When he asked about our other children, I answered, “Two boys.”

Then, I saw him type *LABIA* on the screen. My eyes filled with tears as I grabbed the tech’s arm and locked eyes with him. “Are you serious?” I asked, my voice trembling with amazement.

He chuckled softly, nodding. “Yes!” It felt like a dream come true. I knew it was a girl, but seeing it confirmed filled me with overwhelming joy. The miracle I’d prayed for day after day was right here. It made every tear and painful long night only months prior worth it.

My emotions ebbed and flowed. Some days, I felt calm and let myself feel excited. Other days, worry about the health of this baby crept in. One day, I called my grandmother Mama O to share the news. She was born and raised in Mexico and moved to the U.S. in her twenties after marrying my grandpa. I loved how her warm accent colored her words. I shared that I was having a girl and confessed my worries about her health and development.

In her beautiful accent, Mama O said to me, “Kah-dee-sa, you stop it. God blessed you with this miracle. She is going to be fine!” I cried. Her conviction brought calm over me.

Since I was pregnant, I couldn’t do my usual cancer screenings and was only able to have blood work done. I tried to set aside worries about my health and the baby’s. On good days, I let myself feel excited. I painted the nursery from blue to pink, and I got a new rug, rocker, and bedding. It was really happening! We were so close, and I was counting down the days. Nearly eighty women turned out for Marley’s baby shower. I couldn't believe it. A friend told me, "No one knew this would ever happen—not even you! It's a miracle, and we are so happy for you!" Marley and I were showered with love and blessings.

My C-Section was scheduled. The build up of twenty-five years of anticipation was nearly bursting! The daughter I had always waited for was nearly here. Marley Hope Sherwood made her debut in late January. She was so little—so much smaller than anyone expected her to be—weighing just 4 lbs 9 oz. Her head was still measuring average, so the thought was that her brain kept growing even though her body didn't. I eased and never considered for a moment that Marley's body wouldn't catch up.

She looked like a little baby bird, with a head just a bit bigger than her tiny arms and legs. Nothing we had fit her! She was so small but absolutely perfect to me. We came home after the standard forty-eight hours. As Marley grew, she felt soft and delicate, like a firm jelly in my arms. By six months, she was round and squishy and had adorable white creases between her olive-toned rolls. She was content to play quietly on the floor or in her Bumbo seat on the counter as I cooked. Every day, I dressed her up in bows, necklaces, shoes, and matching outfits. I painted her tiny fingernails and toenails. She'd pull her foot back quickly whenever I tried to paint her toes—a little quirk I found funny. I didn't let it stop me, and I didn't think to be concerned about it.

CHAPTER 3

Noticing

At Marley's six-month checkup, the doctor asked if she was rolling over or sitting up. She wasn't doing either of those things, nor even trying to. The doctor sounded slightly concerned but suggested we check again at her next visit.

When Marley was nine months, the answers were still the same. The doctor recommended contacting the Department of Developmental Disabilities for Early Intervention. I was unfamiliar with that agency, so he explained that by now, Marley should be hitting these milestones. She needed support to strengthen her muscles. He wrote a referral, reassuring me that therapy could help her catch up—a theme that seemed to follow us for years to come.

In early December, a therapist evaluated Marley and diagnosed her with "low tone"—weak muscle tone. She'd need physical therapy for strength, occupational therapy for fine motor skills, and possibly speech therapy. My weekly calendar quickly filled up. Each therapy session was an hour long, occupying three out of the five weekdays. Within weeks, Marley's muscles strengthened, and by eleven months, she could sit up on her own. We were thrilled and hopeful. Maybe she really was catching up!

Her first birthday party was a grand celebration with red, pink, and white cupcakes, and balloons and decorations filling the backyard. Though she could sit up, she needed support nearby because she toppled over easily if she leaned. Her once round frame had grown thin. Therapies began to dominate our lives. For two years, we had three sessions a week. Everything was an uphill battle for Marley. I clung to my vision of a picture-perfect family. After reaching the first milestone of sitting up, we noticed very little progress for the next six months. Therapists cycled in and out. Some I connected with, others I didn't. I resented the constant commitment, and even though I was instructed to practice exercises between sessions, I barely found time as a young mom of three. Each week, I'd realize I hadn't done them. The guilt weighed on me heavily.

Marley's ear infections became constant, and her eyes were often gunky. At sixteen months, we put tubes in her ears and had her tear ducts surgically cleaned. At eighteen months, she was sitting up and rolling over but still not crawling. Watching other babies her age hit milestones left me feeling inadequate, as if somehow it was my fault Marley wasn't hitting those same markers.

Noticing Marley's delays for her age, people would often ask, "What does she have?" One Sunday, a woman at church bluntly asked, "So, what's wrong with her?" I wanted to punch her or, more truthfully, cry. Her words cut so deep. As Marley grew, so did the comments—people confirming that something was "wrong." It made me feel a fierce need to make Marley "right."

In the summertime we were at a family reunion. I laid Marley on a blanket in the lodge. I watched her army crawl and then rise onto her knees, something she'd never done before. I held my breath! She started rocking back and forth, and then it happened! She started crawling! I looked at Josh with watery eyes. She finally turned a corner at the eighteen month marker and started crawling. She walked at two years old. The milestones we hardly gave a second thought to with our boys became huge celebrations with Marley!

Josh and I had wanted our kids close together, but when Marley turned two, I wasn't ready to start trying. She'd just started walking, and mothering her required more than I'd ever experienced with Drey or Crew. ***Should I even try for another baby?*** The decision was mine, and it weighed heavily on me. Our kitchen table had six chairs for five people, and every time I saw that empty chair I'd wonder, ***Is someone supposed to be sitting in that seat?*** Slowly, the quiet wondering became a pull. I knew another little one was meant to occupy that spot.

Six months after Marley's second birthday, I finally felt ready to try for another baby. I got pregnant right away and was thrilled, envisioning a March 2011 due date. Marley and this baby would be three years apart, a bit more than my others, but it felt right giving Marley a little more time to catch up developmentally. Life moved on with doctor visits, therapies for Marley, and sports for Drey and Crew.

That summer, we went to California with Josh's family. I arrived early with the kids and Josh would join us later. As soon as I got to the house, I went to the bathroom and realized I was miscarrying. I went to my room to "take a nap," but I lay on my bed and cried. I'd never known loss like this. There would be no baby in March. When I got back home, I called my OB, who reassured me, "It's OK. This happens often. You can try again next month!" Her response felt dismissive. I wanted answers, not encouragement to try again. I was grieving, and now a new fear of pregnancy loss lingered—if it happened once, how could I be sure it wouldn't happen again?

A couple of months later, I was pregnant again. I felt cautiously optimistic, guarding my heart just in case. I'd miscarried the last time at five or six weeks, so I held my breath, feeling a surge of hope as I passed that mark. With each passing week, I felt more secure. At nine weeks, we shared the news with our families. But then, at ten weeks, I started bleeding and having contractions. *No, not again!*

I felt like running away—not wanting to be home, to face anyone, or hear the "sorries." The physical pain was intense, but my heartache was far worse. I knew what was happening. The pain escalated and we decided to go to the ER. Blood work confirmed the pregnancy, with all levels appearing normal. I was so surprised!

"Sometimes women bleed during pregnancy without miscarrying," the doctor explained. "We'll do an ultrasound to check."

"I don't see anything in there," I expressed to the ultrasound technician. I didn't expect her to say anything back.

"I don't either," she softly replied.

My heart sank. The doctor explained it was a blighted ovum. "It's a miracle any baby is created," he said. "The DNA exchange must be perfect, and sometimes it isn't." In my case, something was growing, producing the right hormones, but no fetus or heartbeat ever formed. My body was tricked into thinking it was nurturing life, but there was nothing there. When it finally recognized this, it tried to expel the mass, and the doctor had to assist. This loss hurt more than the first. Two times now. We drove home in silence, overwhelmed with grief.

The first miscarriage had brought sadness as I thought of the March due date that would never come. This time was different. Heavier. I could barely get out of bed. Life moved on with three little ones to care for plus Marley's therapies, but it felt like the world should have stopped. A cloud of sadness lingered over me each day. Depression ran in my family, and I feared this might be my tipping point. Telling our families about loss *again* felt unbearable. I wanted it all to go away—to pretend it never happened. It was difficult to show up for my kids when all I wanted to do was hide under my covers. This wasn't me; I was a do-er, but now I couldn't bring myself to do anything. September dragged on, and I kept everything inside. *Who would even understand?*

At the end of the month, I visited a naturopath for ozone injections in my knees, which were worn from years of dancing and running. While there, I hesitated, then asked, "Can I talk to you about something else?" Tears filled my eyes. Surprised, he softened, closing the door.

"I don't know what's wrong with me," I confessed, crying. "I've never felt like this before." He gently asked questions, and I shared about my recent miscarriages.

"Oh! That explains it!" he said with empathy and understanding. "Your hormones are out of balance from the miscarriage. I know just what to do to help you!" His reassurance comforted me deeply.

Returning home, I felt like myself again—actually, even better! Whatever this naturopath did had worked! He introduced me to natural healing—herbs, vitamins, and acupuncture—to reset my system. My eyes had been opened to unconventional methods of treatment as well as the body's own healing potential. I became a believer!

In January, I had a positive pregnancy test. In February, I miscarried again. That was three. *What did this mean?* Why did this keep happening? I was done trying. I was done continually getting my heart broken. At the same time, it didn't feel final. Maybe this was how it was supposed to be? Maybe I just needed more time to mend and sort out my feelings?

I got to the year mark of trying to conceive and keep another baby. It was now that I would have been holding one in my arms or at least growing one in my belly. Instead, I had neither. After three consecutive miscarriages, my OB said to call her the next time I got a positive pregnancy test and she would get me on progesterone straightaway. She thought maybe that would help. I was a constant pendulum—hopeful for a successful pregnancy and then haunted by my past three experiences.

In the middle of all this, I had an oversized Tupperware box of sand that stayed under the couch in my living room and crushed Cheerios on the kitchen floor. Textures were Marley's sensory nemesis. For therapy, she would have to play in the sandbox and walk on the Cheerios in hopes of desensitizing her little feet. She would curl up her foot every time Belinda, the occupational therapist, put it in the sand. It wasn't just textures she touched, it was also textures of food. She wouldn't eat certain things and still won't. One day at my parents' house, I was wondering what to make for the kids for lunch. My mom suggested peanut butter and jelly sandwiches. "No," I said, "Marley won't eat that."

"Well, you just give it to her and tell her, 'Tough. That's what's for lunch,'" my mom said with authority. She didn't understand. This wasn't just being "picky"—Marley was different. She couldn't stand sticky peanut butter, rubbery jelly, soft bread, and textures like oatmeal, pudding, or applesauce. Even baby food must have been torture for her. Crunchy, salty foods—chips, crackers, toast—were her favorites, and we gave her whatever she'd eat!

Overwhelmed by life, I allowed myself to confide in a close family member. She showed up later that day with textured rubber balls she heard were good for child development. She offered to come over weekly to help Marley with her exercises. I felt relieved and even cried, but she never did come over again, and I never did remind her. A familiar belief replayed in my mind: *I am alone and have to do everything on my own.*

Marley's appetite continually declined in her second year. I kept nursing her for a time because it was nearly all she would eat. She was so small and weak. She felt like a baby, not at all like a toddler. She nursed in the morning, refused food during the day, and nursed again before bed. She lost weight quickly, becoming even more limp and lifeless. Feeling helpless, I took her to our pediatrician who then referred us to a gastroenterologist. We got in to see him right when Marley turned three. He suggested an endoscopy. My heart broke as I watched her roll away for the procedure.

"She has two ulcers," the doctor told us. *How could a baby have ulcers? Was this my fault?* I felt responsible.

She needed medicine to coat her stomach and a boosted calorie intake. We relied heavily on vanilla Pediasure! The memory of that day-old sippy cup under the bed still makes me gag!

CHAPTER 4

Navigating

Potty training was the next developmental milestone. I tried when she was three, but it was clear she wasn't ready. I paused, despite advice about consistency. I called a woman I knew who had a daughter with similar delays. I was seeking advice about potty training, a pep talk—anything! Her only response was, "Oh Karissa, I don't even know!" I hung up and cried. I was truly on my own. I never called her again.

Waiting was hard, but I trusted my instincts, something I never did! I tried again when she was closer to four. She'd sit on the potty but wouldn't go. One day, knowing she couldn't hold it much longer, I held her over the toilet as she squirmed and resisted.

"Come on, Mar, you can do it! Tinkle in the toilet!" She didn't know how to consciously relax those muscles. "Let the tinkle go in the potty!" I encouraged. Finally, a trickle appeared. She cried and so did I. It scared her, but she did it! Progress was slow, but at least we were moving!

I decided to try for one last pregnancy, telling myself this would be the final attempt. In June, a positive test and a prescription for progesterone filled me with hope. Each week felt like a miracle, and this pregnancy was different—more exhaustion, nausea, and sensitivity to smells. I wondered if this baby might be like Marley and if I'd be able to handle it. I was already juggling so much.

Before the kids were in school all day, I'd take them on daily outings. My hopes were that they'd burn off energy, and I'd get a little break. I ran myself ragged managing the house. I rarely rested, read, or took time for myself. There was too much to do. I often reacted intensely to minor things and questioned why I couldn't control my emotions.

Target was my numbing place. Running errands was what I did to kill time. Once, when I was at Lowe's with all the kids, I saw an acquaintance. "Hi. What are you guys doing here?" he asked.

"Killing time," I heard myself reply. *Wow.* I was waiting for this moment to be over so I could go on to the next. I wasn't present at all. Mothering small children was so hard!

We were told that now that Marley was three, her state services would only continue through Early Intervention—a specialized daily preschool program at a local school. She seemed too young, and I didn't feel either of us was ready, but I ultimately decided to enroll her in the program. Her backpack was almost as big as she was. Her hours were something like 9 a.m. to 2 p.m. While the kids were all at school, I cleaned, did laundry, planned dinner, and ran errands. Once they returned, it was homework, snacks, dinner prep, therapy sessions, and sports practices.

Our mornings were also anything but calm—always a race against the clock. I had a nonnegotiable checklist: beds made, rooms tidied, trash taken out, and dishwasher unloaded. I pushed the boys to hustle, too, all to create some external order, hoping it might bring internal peace. I kept no journals to reflect back on those days; I only have memories. The journals I did keep were filled with light, happy moments—never the hard parts. Even in private journals I still only showed the parts I wanted people to see.

Little Presley arrived in late February. The medications administered for the pain from surgery had always created a barrier between myself and the little soul I just brought into the world. They disconnected me from the realness of my body and the presentness of the special moment. The mother-child bond never happened until later, once the medications wore off and I was back to all my faculties. This time, though, was different. I had just been wheeled into the recovery room with my new little baby. For a moment, there were no nurses coming in and out, no family going back and forth. It was just me and Presley. I looked into her little eyes and my gaze seemed to keep going deeper and deeper. It went all the way ***through*** her. The hazy fog of disorientation parted and this feeling, this knowing, came over me. ***This face,*** I thought, ***I know this face. It is so familiar to me.*** I felt that I already knew this little soul and I instantly bonded with her. We were connected. It felt like a reunion, not a first meeting.

Here she was, my beautiful rainbow baby. Like a rainbow, she represented beauty after a time of darkness. It is said that rainbow babies act as a symbol of renewal and hope. That was Presley. She breathed new life into me. Everything about her was light. Her hair was bright blonde, like the rays of the golden sun. Her brilliant blue eyes reflected the light in everything around her. Her sheer existence radiated light. When she was little, I often joked and told her that I should have named her Sunny instead because she was always sunny and bursting with light!

I could immediately tell she was different from Marley—her muscles were stronger, and her latch was intense! Despite nursing three other babies, Presley's latch was the most challenging, and each feeding was painful. Nursing every couple of hours meant I couldn't always keep an eye on the now four-year-old Marley. Even with a newborn baby, I was still on high alert. Keeping Marley safe was a full-time job! She was a natural escape artist. I couldn't leave the room for a second without her disappearing. She loves freedom and the space to explore. Curiosity fuels her. She is constantly driven for new stimuli—one that I often could not give her.

Marley, the Escape Artist

We installed latches at the top of every door leading outside to keep Marley in and safe. It worked—until she figured out she could push a chair over to reach the latch. I was constantly asking the boys to go out and look for her, something they tired of quickly. Sometimes, I'd find her by the mailboxes near the main road or in Josh's yard where construction materials and workers were constantly coming and going. Once, I found her petting a horse in a neighbor's pen, rubbing its belly!

When Marley was nine, I found her sneaking toward a neighbor's horse in their pasture. I yelled, and thankfully, she came back. A few days later, I thought she'd gone with Josh to drop Drey off at a football game. When Josh returned without her, I panicked and asked, "Where's Marley? I thought she was with you!"

Josh said he'd sent her back in to stay with me, but she hadn't come inside. We rushed to the pasture and saw her just feet from a horse, approaching from behind. As we yelled for her to stop, she moved farther away from us. It felt like slow motion, and we stood on edge, fearing the worst. The horse got spooked, and thankfully ran away instead of kicking Marley, but she continued to chase it! This cycle continued until Crew was able to reach her after dashing across the pasture.

Another time, when she was ten, after I'd called around and no one had seen her, I found her bike outside a family member's house around the corner. The house sat alone with no other homes around it. I knew they weren't home. I walked past a crew of construction workers painting the home's exterior. They would have seen this tiny, little girl—all alone—ride past them and go into what appeared to be an empty house. The garage was open with no sign of cars. My heart beat faster and faster with every new possible piece of danger I gathered. I walked in to find Marley and our little dog, Minnie, sitting unharmed with the family member's bulldog. I breathed a huge sigh of relief!

Each time I find her in a dangerous situation, I wonder, *Is this it? Is this the day?* Marley has no fear or understanding of risk. I often rely on her angels because I can't protect her alone. I need every minute of the six hours she is at school—where I know she is safe—for my system to rest. It is the only time my body gets rest during the waking hours of each day.

Challenges with Marley

The therapists noticed that Marley often stared off when they started working with her. "She might be having staring spells, or absence seizures," one said. It didn't go anywhere. I didn't do research, and they didn't say much more than that.

It was brought up again when she was six. This time, it was recommended that we see a neurologist. We had seen many of them over the years regarding Marley's development, but none of them had any answers. In regard to these staring spells, an MRI showed abnormal brain activity, though it was inconclusive for seizures. The anti-seizure medication, Keppra, was prescribed, and it was awful! Marley turned into someone unrecognizable—screaming, crying uncontrollably, and slamming doors. It was distressing for all of us, and she seemed miserable too! We hoped her behavior would level out with time.

The summer she was eight, I took the kids to a family beach house. Josh joined us on the weekends. It was a low point for me, and Marley's behavior mirrored my struggle. She cried every day, and despite the challenges, I stayed, thinking, *Tomorrow will be better*. Life at home felt so much harder than life at the beach. Marley cried the whole time on an outing to the zoo. The next day the kids and I wheeled her to the beach in a wagon. She didn't last long and we wheeled her all the way back to the house. Something was wrong. I didn't know what, and she couldn't tell me! I thought it might be her ears. A local doctor there in California confirmed double ear infections. This was the constant cycle of our lives in many ways: throwing paint on the wall to see what would stick, barely surviving while pretending we were living life.

Another summer we rented an RV and took a family road trip to Colorado. Normally, Marley loves trips and car rides, but this trip she screamed and cried the whole way there. I felt helpless and powerless, two common emotions I have had my entire life. Marley's circumstances continued to feed these feelings.

Disciplining Marley and finding consequences for her is something Josh and I were never good at. The boys often asked why she didn't have the same consequences. "Mom, that's not fair." And they're right, but it's not the same playing field with Marley.

Once, a boy encouraged Marley to repeat profanities and racial slurs, recording her as she did. Our son was furious! While our son was reaming out this friend, his anger was quickly diverted to Marley—she was keying his car! He had tried to do something nice—including her by bringing her along—and he regretted it terribly! We all reach breaking points with Marley. She can be impulsive and obsessive. She'll slap you in frustration and sincerely apologize seconds later. She'll promise not to ride her scooter out the gate, only to do it again two hours later. She can't grasp the concept of consequences and can't solve problems. It's challenging; sometimes we laugh, and other times we cry. The boys' frustration is equally understandable—it's hard on everyone in our family, not just me and Josh.

Struggles in Motherhood

I dedicated my life to being a mother; my identity was completely tied to being a mom and wife. Where I come from, sacrificing personal wants and needs for your children is praised. I gave them everything, knowing no other way. I didn't know what I liked or wanted outside of motherhood; it never crossed my mind.

* When Presley was seven months old, I was asked to lead a youth group for girls ages twelve to eighteen at our church. I dove in wholeheartedly, loving the constant activity and the focus on others. It was easier to look outward than to focus on my own life. I felt "good" by "saving" others—these girls, friends, and family. It gave me a sense of purpose. I don't know how I managed it all: Marley was four, my boys were seven and nine, and Presley was a nursing baby. Marley's therapies were three times a week—all after school—and I dedicated countless hours to the youth program. Though exhausting, this leadership role kept me from admitting my own struggles, which I didn't know how to navigate or share with others.

Once, after a meeting, two women from our leadership turned to me and asked, "What can we do for you? What do you need?" These questions caught me so off guard that I didn't know how to respond. I didn't even know what my needs were! I felt my eyes fill with tears, but all I could say was, "I don't know," and then quickly steer the conversation back to the youth program.

No one around me ever talked about the hard stuff; it just wasn't what you did. You talked about the good, kept smiling, and kept moving forward, all while cleaning out this drawer or that one. I never acknowledged my own pain, not even quietly, though it was always there.

* At six years old, Marley had to be re-evaluated for eligibility by DDD (Department of Developmental Disabilities). At the time, we had full funding for all of her therapies, doctor appointments, and regular scans of any kind. If she qualified for long-term care, she would continue to receive services until she was eighteen years old. If she did not qualify, her state services would be discontinued. The process of paperwork and forms to fill out was unreal, and DDD didn't have to do all the heavy lifting—I did! It was draining, overwhelming, and emotionally taxing. I had to give complete documentation of health history, doctors, procedures, delays and concerns, school records, and all situations where she had been at high risk or in danger. There was evaluation after evaluation by teachers and school psychologists. The list went on and on! It took me months to comb through it all. I had heard how hard it was to qualify, and I knew many parents had gone through this same process just to be denied. Having the support of funding for Marley's care alleviated a huge part of the burden—not the whole thing but definitely a part. I had to get her qualified, and somehow I did!

* We lived on a street with my husband's family. There were almost a dozen cousins with only a year or two between each of them. They grew up more like siblings than cousins. It was an incredible

support system—one that Marley, of all people, needed but couldn't fully experience. She couldn't attend the same school as the others because our local school didn't have a program for her. I had to drop her off at a separate school every day. The separation was hard; I wondered what message it sent her. I cried the first day, feeling she didn't belong in her assigned program. But where else could she go? The daily drives were not only physically tiring but also mentally and emotionally draining. One day, my sister-in-law offered to drop Marley off at her school during carpool. I cried. And I accepted her help—a rare thing for me. Though I needed support, I struggled to ask for it or even to receive it when it was extended toward me.

* Once, a sitter—trying to wrangle Marley—cried to the kids, "I don't know how your mom does this every day! This is so hard!" I felt sad because I didn't know if she'd ever come back. I also felt extremely validated.

* I have always had a "tomorrow is a new day" mindset, but the way I reacted in stressful situations felt completely out of my control. Sometimes I would already "fail" by 8 a.m. I could not step back, take a breath, and then go back in with a clear head. I always hoped that one day I would magically wake up and be able to do life differently. I always wondered what was wrong with me.

* Josh's family were never dog people, and certainly no one ever had a dog in the house, so you can imagine my complete shock when my father-in-law approached me and said, "Karissa, I really think Marley needs a little dog, one that she can take care of, that she can hold when she is sad and sleep with at night."

My jaw dropped. A dog? In the house? On her bed? I stared at him in shock. I had no room in my life for a dog, and I didn't know anything about them. He brought it up a couple more times. I let the idea ruminate for well over a year. I finally decided I would try it for Marley and we parlayed the dog into the kids' Christmas present. We got a little Yorkie, named her Cocoa, and presented her to the kids in a beautiful box on Christmas morning. She peed in the pretty box right as the kids lifted her out. And so it began.

Why did I get a puppy? Cocoa was a constant worry, another "child" to watch. Marley loved her at times but would also impulsively toss, squeeze, or kick her. I think Marley liked being bigger than something. I was always either scolding Cocoa or trying to protect her. This beautiful visual my father-in-law had painted for me completely backfired. I finally decided to rehome Cocoa.

At the same time, Marley's behavior was through the roof. At home, we couldn't tell at all if the meds were helping. Her teacher said she thought the meds helped Marley focus better at school, though she couldn't speak to the staring spells; it was too hard to tell if it was helping those. That wasn't enough for us. After two years, we decided to take Marley off the anti-seizure meds.

CHAPTER 5

A Voice

The only involvement I required of Josh with the kids' schools was to accompany me to Marley's annual IEP meetings. I really needed his support. I was a mess each time—crying before, during, and after. These meetings were isolating and I took them so critically. They were filled with comments like, "Your child can't do this," "She's far behind," and "She needs more support." Marley was adorable, and her teachers loved helping her, but her dependency left her without confidence or a sense of personal pride. Marley's progress felt stagnant, and I worried she was capable of more. I wondered constantly if we should switch her to our local school where she'd be with Crew and her cousins. Josh and I weighed the pros and cons, considering whether she might thrive with a paraprofessional in general education. The school year's end was approaching, and a change felt possible.

After a string of phone calls, the final verdict from the superintendent was, "There is no evidence to support that she will be successful there, so the answer is no." We were shocked! This was *our* daughter and they were telling us what we could and could not do with her? I had never realized how much power our education system has.

After asking around, we found a lawyer who advocated for children like Marley. She gathered all the information and said we would have to revisit everything when school was back in. I had no idea how long this whole process was. I waited the whole summer hoping, but not knowing how things would shake out.

I am grateful for the summer of waiting. It gave me time to experiment with the new-to-me concept of manifesting that I had recently learned. I knew deep down that this was the right move for Marley. I lived in the vibration, or feeling, that this change was already confirmed. I bought red, white, and blue uniforms for the new school before we ever had the meeting. I made necklaces in the same colors to coordinate with each outfit. I visualized her there. I imagined dropping her off in the morning at school with all of her cousins. I pictured her getting out of the car so proudly, wearing her new backpack. I felt her there. I never doubted the change would come, and I lived as if it were already so.

Marley returned to the same program with the same teacher when school started again. We had to keep carrying on like this until the meeting. It was so uncomfortable dropping her off at school, knowing that her current teacher was aware of the change we wanted to make. The teacher had always spoken with a soft, sweet voice and treated Marley and me with kindness. With our circumstances now changing, so was she! I saw a side of her I hadn't ever experienced before. Her voice was still soft and sweet, but she spewed passive-aggressive jabs that criticized my choice, my parenting, Marley's capabilities, and the credibility of the program Marley would be in if the change was approved.

I let all of her jabs occupy some place in me. One day, while pondering on all this, I could "see" energetic "cords" between this teacher and me. Each cord represented a comment she had spoken about me behind my back. I chose to "pull" them all out. They "looked" like cords but felt like daggers. I cried pulling out each one. I was crushed and shocked that she would turn on me so quickly and harshly. It felt like betrayal, and that was painfully familiar. I never jabbed back at her, mostly because I hated confrontation. Instead, I always kept everything inside. I sat and stewed on all the things I woulda, coulda, and shoulda said to stand up for myself.

The paperwork was all in order, schedules finally aligned, and the long-awaited meeting between the school counselor, the lawyer, the school psychologist, the teachers, and Josh and me was officially set for September of that year. On the day of the meeting, I walked in sweaty-palmed, my heart pounding against my chest. I was cordial and polite but wanted minimal interaction with the primary teacher. I could barely make eye contact with her. From the outside looking in, the scene appeared to be that of a brave mother fighting for her voiceless daughter—and it was. It was also so much more than that. In hindsight, the burning fire that fueled my fight was actually for the little me. I was fighting for the parts of little Karissa who didn't get her needs met, who couldn't speak up for herself, couldn't communicate or express what she wanted, and who most of the time didn't even know what her needs were. Marley's circumstances with the school strummed a deep wound in me that I was unaware of. I didn't want Marley to feel how I felt, so I forced myself to stand up and speak up.

I could have cut the tension in the room with a knife. These were all faces I had interacted with consistently for four years—from IEP meetings to evaluations to daily interactions—for Marley. We were all supposed to be on the same team, and now I felt the complete opposite was happening. Each face was playing nice to a degree but not being completely honest. Each said their concerns were all for the highest good of Marley, but it didn't feel that way. The school was tiptoeing to protect themselves and their agenda. I also tiptoed in my own way. I spoke the truth of my feelings while also softening them to keep the others as "comfortable" as I could. I was never one to rock the boat. I didn't address how dismissed and betrayed I felt. I couldn't personally leave it *all* on the table!

Marley's advocate was no-nonsense in the meeting. She was direct and knew our child's rights inside and out. For what felt like hours, we went around and around in the meeting as both sides voiced their concerns. With nothing else to discuss, the meeting ended and we were told we would hear from someone soon with a decision. As we left the classroom and walked toward our car, I felt something I had never felt before. It was the stirring of my own voice! I had never really used it before. Up until this moment, I didn't know I could! I felt blood moving through me in a new way. I felt alive! I felt strong and empowered with a new sense of pride. I did for Marley what she could not do for herself. I did for little Karissa what she couldn't do for herself back then either.

A week later, the advocate phoned. Marley was granted the right to switch to her home school! She would repeat second grade in a mainstream classroom, go out for generals, and share a paraprofessional with one other girl. The switch would be made right after fall break. I was overcome with emotions. I had played a huge part in this! I used the law of manifesting, and it worked. I used my voice, and it was heard. I was creating change. Wow! I was starting to see myself and my life with new eyes. Maybe I was a creator!

Fall break came to a close. The kids would be returning to school, but it felt like the first day of school for Marley. I asked if all the kids would come out front for "first day of school" photos. It was an electric feeling to see her dressed in the same red, white, and blue uniforms, taking pictures with all of her cousins. My eyes watered behind my sunglasses as I dropped all of the kids off to school. Before this day, I had seen this whole scene in my mind many times. Marley jumped out of the car wearing her new backpack—and had a huge smile across her face. She was one of them. She belonged. I felt a sense of belonging too.

Each year from second to fourth grade, the gap between Marley and her peers widened, despite my hopes it would narrow. In IEP meetings, I saw her peers' work alongside Marley's attempts at simple math. By fourth grade, her teacher admitted she was giving Marley busy work because Marley couldn't keep up. It stung, but it was true. Over those few years, we had gradually adjusted her IEP to increase her time in special ed and decrease her mainstream class time.

In fifth grade the SPED teacher was Mr. Miller. We knew him from our days at the other school, and Marley loved him! He and Marley vibed so well together. After the first few days of the new school year, he said something to me like, "Marley doesn't want to go sit with Mrs. Smith's class for lunch, but I know you want her to." I had to take a step back and pause for a moment. I finally saw how, for so many years, I had made Marley's life about *me*—how I wanted it to look because it was a reflection of me. I wanted her to belong with the crowd that was average. I wanted her to fit in with those who were more readily accepted. I could finally see it all in a way I hadn't before. I was finally able to let Marley just be who she was and not who I needed her to be!

Marley wanted to stay where she was more comfortable, and that was with Mr. Miller's class. He was probably surprised when I said, "Yes, I am totally OK with that. I want Marley to be wherever *she* wants to be." I really did feel that way. For the ten years prior, I hadn't. The circumstances of her life no longer hooked me the way they always had before. This was a new feeling! After a few more days, Mr. Miller checked back in. He shared that Marley was wanting to go back to the mainstream class for less time each day. "What do you want me to do?" he asked.

"It's totally OK," I said. These conversations continued until she wasn't going to the mainstream class at all. She was only participating in PE and art with the general education class. She slowly transitioned into the self-contained classroom full-time at the elementary school for fifth and sixth grade. She has been in this type of program ever since. Presently, Marley is seventeen years old and in her tenth grade year. I still feel that it was the right choice to move schools and programs even though in the end, it turned out that the special education program was exactly where she belonged. For a decade, I battled that, unable and unwilling to accept it for so long.

I once thought that the only way to feel free was for the situation to change. I attached joy, peace, and liberation to a particular outcome, and that is why I suffered. *Could I really be OK if this was our life? Could I really be OK with things staying exactly as they were?* The answer is *yes*—but yes is a choice.

CHAPTER 6

The Unraveling

Unravel: to take apart, undo, destroy

One summer, I took up pilates with a couple of the moms on my street. The studio was close enough that we'd jog there while we chatted, take our class, and then jog home. One day, in the early morning sun as we got closer to home, I saw an image by our mailboxes on the main road that I didn't register right away. As I got closer, I saw two little girls in nightgowns and messy hair. They were ***my*** little girls! As soon as I recognized them, I cried out, "Can I not have anything?!" I couldn't hold my feelings in! I used to do it so well. They just burst out of me!

I was getting up at 4:30 a.m.—in the summer mind you—to get some time in for myself, to move my body and get my mind right before the kids woke up and needed me. This was *my* time and now it wasn't even mine. ***What now? I have to get up at 3 a.m.? 2 a.m.? You've got to be kidding me!*** I cried the rest of the walk home. I felt like a prisoner of my life's circumstances. I have to be on watch all of the time! What little freedom I felt I had was stripped from me. Pile on the frustration, anger, and resentment! This was my reality, and I was stuck in it.

My digestive system never was the same after having surgery for stomach cancer. When Marley was seven—the year before we changed schools—the pains I occasionally had in my stomach grew more frequent and intensified in severity. When the pains would come on, usually I could go to bed early and by morning I'd feel better. One night the pain became excruciating. Nothing I tried made it subside. None of my go-tos were helping. It was a new sensation of pain in my stomach that I was not accustomed to. We debated going to the hospital. *What if they turn me away? What if it's nothing? What could this be?*

"This isn't just *nothing,*" Josh said. "You are clearly in so much pain. If you knew they wouldn't turn you away, would you still go? Do you really feel like something is wrong?"

I sobbed and said, "Yes."

"Well, there's our answer," he said.

I felt trapped in my own body, desperate to escape the pain. I knew something was seriously wrong but didn't trust myself over the doctors. As soon as I was in the exam room, I vomited my entire dinner. Pain meds didn't help until they gave me the strongest they had. Their plan was to start with base level testing: an ultrasound. I felt defeated and frustrated—why weren't they listening to me or reviewing my past history? The problem felt urgent, but I didn't advocate for myself like I wish I would have.

I didn't like shuffling the kids all over, so I assured Josh I was OK to be at the hospital without him so he could be home with our four young kids. *Why did I do that?* Self-abandoning was something familiar. I was at the hospital for days with no further findings from tests. Everything came back negative or normal. I was on heavy pain meds my whole stay there. The cold, dark, isolating hospital room stirred up feelings of loneliness and depression. It was horrible. I'd try to get out of my room and walk the hospital floor for a slight change in scenery. I always paused and looked out the big window overlooking the dried cornfields that faced the direction of home. Why was I stuck *here* when everyone I love is *there*? My real life felt so far away, so much farther than the distant span of dry fields between us. I'd think about my kids. *What are they doing at this moment? Do they miss me as much as I miss them?* The separation was almost unbearable. I was frustrated and confused and in so much pain. I ate minimally because my body seemed to be happier without food. The IV kept me hydrated and I stuck to soups, unless I was required to fast for another test.

One day in the hospital, while drifting in and out of consciousness, I saw my great-grandmother Abuelita standing at the foot of my bed with her brother. She looked young, just like in an old photo, and though they said nothing, their presence filled me with love and comfort, reassuring me I wasn't alone in that cold, dark hospital room. Abuelita died when I was eight, but she left a lasting mark on me. I felt deeply connected to her despite the language barrier. It made perfect sense she'd visit me now. Later, back home, I wondered if it had really happened, but it felt too real to dismiss as a dream.

Each test just gave my body more time to unravel. By day five, we were still waiting on one last test. Feeling utterly broken, I sobbed to Josh. After expressing our frustration, I was finally allowed to go home with plans to complete the test as an outpatient. Relief was short-lived—I was back in the hospital two days later. The test revealed a bowel obstruction, which led to emergency surgery; hours after receiving that test result, I was opened up straight down my middle.

My insides were literally twisted in knots from the surgical juncture nine years prior, physically mirroring the emotional unraveling I'd felt for years. I spent the rest of the week recovering in the hospital with a familiar NG tube in my nose and strips of surgical tape all the way down the long incision on my abdomen. On one of the doors, I saw the cutest handwriting in black dry erase marker. The boys had written me notes when they had come to visit.

"Mom, I'm glad you didn't die of cancer."

"Mom, come home soon."

"Mom, Marley says she loves you."

Friends and family came to visit and take me on walks around the floor to get me up and moving. One day, my mom came and asked what she could do for me. I said, "Can you wash my hair?" It was such a simple thing but something I needed and couldn't do on my own. I felt like a young girl again. My mom tenderly washed, brushed, and braided my hair. It meant so much to me. I had decided to take out the extensions that I wore in my hair. It was already long, so why did I feel I needed it to be longer? I said goodbye to them and never had them put in again. Strangely, I took a piece of myself back when I let them go.

I came home to my four children, ages twelve, ten, seven, and three. "Hard" doesn't even begin to describe what that time was like. I could barely move, overwhelmed by pain and the needs of my kids. Meeting even their basic needs on my own was nearly impossible for a very long time. The doctor said the recovery would take three months, with only 1% improvement each day. He was right, and I was unprepared. I went in with stomach pain and left bedridden with a long incision down my belly. Watching other moms go about their lives—working out, shopping, running carpools—I ached to be one of them. "Full recovery" and "normal" seemed light-years away. This already overwhelmed mother continued to drown in her new reality.

A couple of times a week, Josh's sister would text offering to feed the kids dinner. I'd holler and tell them to run down there. One day, the boys broke down in tears—they didn't want to leave. They'd rather be home, even with nothing to eat, than keep being shuffled around. I cried with them. My days dragged on in survival mode. I managed simple breakfasts and sent the kids to school to buy lunch. There were no home-cooked meals, no extra activities—only the basics. We hired help for cleaning and laundry, which made me feel even less capable than the other moms around me. I was the only one in constant need of help, and I hated it!

Summer came and I was still healing, only 1% better each day. It was nice to not have a school schedule, but having the kids home all day was a different kind of hard. I couldn't take them anywhere or do anything. I couldn't even walk out and sit with them at the pool. The boys were OK on their own, but I couldn't let Mar or Presley out alone. Family helped where they could. I was two months post surgery. I pushed my body beyond what it was ready to do and always paid for it. My body pushed back and said, *no, this is too much*. I'd back off for a few days and try again, with the same results. It was so hard to be patient and wait.

Three months came and went. *I should be all better by now.* Technically, I was physically healing from the surgery, but why did I not *feel* any better? I felt so off, so unlike myself—or the self I had once known. The months continued and I felt the same. I had follow-up appointments and expressed my concerns to my doctors. I was told it would just take time for my body to adjust to the changes. This felt like more than that. They were missing something. I knew it but didn't know what that thing was. They weren't listening to me. I felt unheard and dismissed.

I sat crying on the floor of my bathroom one day, throwing a pity party for myself. I remember saying to myself, to God, to and whomever else was on the other end listening, "Why does it feel like the dark, heavy clouds are just over my house? I look around and the sun is shining everywhere else but on me." I sat there in a puddle of despair when moments later, Presley came waltzing into my bathroom, her soft golden curls bouncing off her shoulders. I looked up through my tears and saw her little face. *Sunny—my sun.* It was a beautiful reminder that the sun never did stop shining on me. I had been putting all my focus on the clouds, so I didn't even notice the sun. My lens changed and I felt relief for a moment.

Over time, my mind grew even more cloudy and confused. My thoughts turned dark, and I wondered, *Who am I now? Where did I go?* The person I was becoming felt raw and unfiltered—so unlike the poised, proper version of myself I'd always shown. It was foreign, confusing, but also strangely liberating. I didn't care about the things I once did; caring simply took too much energy.

Darkness consumed me daily, wearing down every part of me. Despair gnawed at me, and on my darkest days, I just wanted to escape, to wake up free from this pain. Thoughts of leaving everything—even my family—crept in. For the first time, I understood mothers who walk away or end their lives. It's not about not caring; it's about enduring something so excruciating that it feels *unbearable.* It's the feeling of, *I can't live like this anymore.*

On these days, the light would peek through the clouds for just a moment, and my great-grandmother Abuelita would speak to me. She'd wrap me up in the warmest light of her love and tell me to hold on and not give up. She said she would help me. I would sob, feeling my hopelessness and despair melt into comfort and reassurance. It was so real. She was right there. I felt her. I heard her. The brightest light came and scooped me up off of the dark floor of hopelessness I was lying on. An overpowering feeling of divine love washed all over me. It was a feeling I had forgotten and missed terribly! The interventions kept me hanging on, clinging to the hope that this was not my forever.

PART 2

HIDDEN CHAMBERS

We are intricate, highly complex beings, and yet we often only identify with that which we can see and feel. Along with the physical body, we are also composed of mental, emotional, and spiritual energetic bodies. The body's main function on each layer is *always* survival.

On a physical level, we involuntarily take over 20,000 breaths of air daily. Once a meal is consumed, we take little to no thought as to what happens to it. Our immune response heightens or multiplies when it senses something foreign and out of order. Our vital organs strive to carry out their respective functions day in and day out, constantly keeping us alive.

Survival on the mental and emotional layers of our energetic body looks like self-preservation. These layers are constantly scanning for danger, averting threats in all forms to continually find ways to keep us *safe*. Our minds have the ability to block out memories of experiences that were particularly distressing or even alter them slightly to make them more pleasant to reflect on. When our hearts get hurt, a part of us creates energetic walls or barriers as a form of protection. I heard the analogy once that dealing with the heart is much like touching a hot stove: once we touch it and feel the burn, we instantly recoil and make a personal vow to never do that again. We learn through our own experience that when we did that thing—let someone in, trusted someone, engaged in that relationship, allowed ourselves to be vulnerable—we got hurt. Walls serve a double purpose: they keep things out but also prevent anything from getting in.

Behind the smile, the polished children, and the home-cooked meals, I had quiet, hidden chambers of my heart that I tucked away and rarely accessed. I knew I couldn't *go there* because I didn't know how to do it without completely falling apart. *Who would want to do that? I didn't have time for that*. It seemed better to just keep the lid on!

When I felt big emotions come, I would push them down and make myself busy. But we all know what happens to a covered pot when it boils for too long. I would lose control in some way: yell at the kids in frustration, burst into tears, or stew with rage over the words of someone that hurt me. After a while, it seemed like the feeling would pass and I'd put the lid back on that pot. I knew no other way.

My friend recently joked, "What is everyone so busy doing all of the time?" We laughed because we knew it was true. The carpools, school projects, Costco runs, laundry, meal prep—the list goes on—some of it is necessary, yes, but quite often we create more of the very things we often loathe and complain about. *Why?* Because this busyness is a form of self-preservation. It is a tool our brain uses to distract and avoid in hopes of protecting. Staying busy kept me from deeply feeling what lived just below my surface. A part of me was constantly trying to keep my mind engaged in all the tasks at hand. We've all heard or used the phrase, "keep my mind off of it." *What does that mean?* It's when we do something to distract us from the emotional places a part of us often goes. I was avoiding, running away from these heavy emotions I didn't know what to do with. They were so much bigger than me and when they came up and crashed over me, they seemed to swallow me whole. I didn't know how to manage the hold and power they had over me.

This busyness I felt I *had* to do to keep up with life worked really well for years. The constant checklist to complete kept me distracted most of the time. It gave me something to outwardly focus on instead of dealing with my inner pain. I never stopped or sat down to rest. I was exhausted all the time, always burning the candle at both ends. Then, mix in a sweet little girl who was not growing and developing like the average child *should*. It was the perfect storm. You wouldn't ever know it, though, unless I let you into every chamber of my heart.

CHAMBER 1

Overwhelm & Fear

I wasn't present to the feeling of overwhelm until I became a mother. My first recollection of having this feeling is when I was in the hospital after having Drey. Thinking of all of my new tasks ahead while caring for a fragile human, myself, and my spouse instantly left me drowning in overwhelm. It intensified with every child that followed. There were always more of them and still only one me.

One dictionary describes ***overwhelm*** as, "to bury or drown beneath a huge mass." Another is "defeat completely." Yes to both. I was drowning, feeling buried, and I was most definitely defeated. I always had so much to do and always felt so behind in life. The list was my own, yes, but I didn't feel I had a choice in it. I had to be a ***good mom***, and it seemed that this way of life was the how. I had no control over Marley's circumstances or the knots I held inside, so I tried to control everything else around me without ever consciously knowing why.

To survive, overdrive was the only speed I knew. I was constantly buried under all the daily tasks waiting to be completed, so my wheels were always spinning. As soon as my eyes opened in the morning, I felt like I was on the clock and I could not clock out until I laid my head on my pillow and closed my eyes again at night. I set my alarm for early morning so I could have some time to myself before the kids were up. It never felt long enough. I overexerted and overextended myself every day for years, all in hopes of being good enough for the people I loved most. I put notes in lunches, made beds that had been left unmade, and kept bins and drawers all orderly. I would even iron the top sheet that folded over the boys' comforter because it had a funny wrinkle in it that always bothered me. It didn't lie *perfectly.*

I wasn't good enough by my own standards. I didn't love myself, so no amount of *good* things I did would ever be enough to fill the hole in my heart. I said yes to everything because I thought I had to. I overcommitted and overextended to numb my pain. It worked sometimes, but it also just fed my overwhelm. It was a vicious cycle. I was on edge all the time. My nerves were frayed, sticking out on end like they were in a permanent state of electrocution. I felt like they needed to be dipped in some kind of hot wax to coat the wired ends. I had no idea how to do this. *How does one smooth or soothe frayed nerves?*

I got big and brave one day and tried to talk to my mom about it, feeling like we had arrived at some kind of common ground. I delivered my detailed nerve visual—what I felt like inside—and then I said, "I think you know what that feels like."

She looked at me like I had ten heads. She had no idea what I was talking about. I could see that she was so disconnected from her body, she didn't know herself in that way at all. She didn't have any awareness of why she operated the way she did when we were young.

She and I didn't even see my childhood the same way. My vulnerability was for nothing. I felt invalidated and overexposed.

Crushed, I asked, "Um, were you even there?" We painted completely different pictures of my childhood. *How was that possible? How could two people who'd been in the same place at the same time see or remember things so differently?* My mother and I had completely different lenses. It was a shocking discovery.

Speaking up gets you nowhere, I told myself after this conversation. I guess all I can do is keep putting one foot in front of the other. I've also realized as I've reflected on this difference in lenses that a part of my mother was not really present during my childhood. She was so wrapped up in her own pain, she couldn't really see or feel what was happening with me. The one person I kind of felt safe enough to open up to in that moment said she did not relate, and that indirectly invalidated my feelings.

When my kids were young, my nervous system response to overwhelm was *fight*. I kept trying to push through, go faster and faster, with the feeling of 500-pound weights on my back. The list was so big that there wasn't enough time to do everything on it, but I would still try. I always felt behind, seldom on top of, and never ahead. This fed the constant feeling of "lack" that I lived in.

Later on in life, my response to overwhelm changed to *freeze*. I wouldn't take any action at all. I think it was my body's way of saying, "No more. We can't keep going like this anymore." I didn't know where to start, so I didn't start anywhere. I shut down on the inside. I would often say, "later," but later wouldn't come until the feeling lifted. I would always say, "Too much!" The kids, the house, the meals—it was all too much! The parent-teacher conferences, the appointments, the therapies—too much! "Too much" is my cue. I haven't rid myself of this coping mechanism, but now I can see it for what it is. It doesn't take much before all I want to do is shut down. The thought I have after the feeling comes is always, *I want to crawl in my bed and pull the covers over my head*! Energetically, that is exactly what I do. I go into *sleep* mode.

What is your typical response to overwhelm? Are you more fight, flight, freeze, or fawn?

How do you recognize your response? What verbiage do you use or what actions do you take?

Why do you think your brain and body respond to stressors this way?

Can you see anywhere in your early life how that coping mechanism might have developed?

Has it changed over the years, or has it always been the same?

If it has changed, why do you think that is?

"But fear doesn't need doors and windows. It works from the inside." —Andrew Clements, *Things Not Seen*

I held volumes of fears I never spoke of. I didn't want to give any of it life, so I tucked it all away. I didn't know what else to do. I would get stuck on thought loops that fed my fears. The only thing that worked to distract my mind was to dive into some kind of busyness. I was kind and sweet and soft spoken. That felt true but not completely true. No one could see what I felt inside because I never let them. Ego is the part of us that wants the world to see us a certain way. I didn't want to be seen as this crazy, uptight, overbearing, controlling mother that could fly off the handle at any moment. It's not a good look. I could *control* that part of me in public usually, but I couldn't always control it at home.

From the outside looking in, I appeared to have it all together. But from the inside looking out, I was a broken mess held together with fake eyelashes and sheer lipgloss. I wasn't trying to fool anyone but myself. I wanted and needed to hear that I was great, going above and beyond, and that I was more than enough. I thrived on external validation. I believed for years that external praise determined value. I thought if I heard it so many times maybe it would start to feel true. It never did.

Our home is where I received instant gratification. My eyes could take a quick scan of any area of our house and provide me a feeling of order and control. This happened on the contrary as well. Disarray heightened my internal chaos. It might take staying up all night or waking up super early, but it could all be done. All of the energy I had was put into everything outside of me. I didn't feel like I could show up in any way other than *perfect*. I thought that performance determined worth and value.

"Insecurity's best cover is perfectionism. That's where it becomes an art form." —Beth Moore, *So Long Insecurity: You've Been a Bad Friend to Us*

I was painfully insecure about everything! I tied my identity to perfection in order to protect my heart from being hurt. Criticism was my recoil. I couldn't give anyone a reason to critique. This was my way to *survive*. I hid behind the mask of perfection for years.

Fear, not love, was the driver. I feared criticism and failure. I feared Marley being criticized because then I would be too. There was nothing I could do to make her perfect or *normal*. No amount of anything I did would be enough to *fix* her. I couldn't help her develop faster. I couldn't make her brain fire differently, but I didn't know that just yet, so I tried! I damn-sure tried with all of the doctors appointments and therapies. I thought surely all of this would do the trick.

I feared abandonment. I felt if I was an angry, short-tempered mother that didn't fulfill her duties to God and family, then the people I loved most would leave me and I would be a complete failure. I could not let that happen! All I wanted was a close family. I couldn't be the reason for it being otherwise! I can see how much I overcompensated, trying to make up in places I could for the places I couldn't.

We can do the same things being driven, motivated, or fueled by very different energies: fear versus love. Take prayer, for example. Have you ever been the fearful parent, so worried about your child and their path that you beg, pray, and plead with God for some kind of mercy or intervention? Do you remember a time doing this? Can you find that feeling? Fear was driving your prayer.

Now let's switch. Same child, same circumstance, same efforts in a prayer but now driven by love. What words would you find? What language would you use? How do you feel offering up a prayer of love for your child? Can you recognize the difference in your body between fear and love, any kind of sensation at all? This is how the body communicates—through sensations. Fear restricts the breath and creates heaviness in the body, primarily in the chest, shoulders, and belly. Love is expansive and creates more space, ease, and settling. With love, energetic weight lifts and we tend to feel lighter.

I read scripture stories to the kids every morning while they ate breakfast. They hated it and really, so did I! It wasn't easy and it wasn't well received. All it brought in was more chaos. It was just one more thing "to do" on my long morning checklist, but I still did it. I *had* to! Day after day I did it out of fear, not love, because I was so afraid of "losing" them—losing my bond, my connection, and my relationship with my children. I was afraid of losing the eternal family unit I had been promised if I lived up to certain requirements. My faith of origin taught me that this was the way to keep them close.

One day, when Drey was in kindergarten, I sent a panicked text to my sister-in-law who was driving our kids to school. "I didn't pray with the kids today! Will you please say a prayer with them before you drop them off?"

"Yes, of course!" she kindly replied.

Fear, not love. I could not miss one day. In short, just remember that fear restricts and love expands.

What fears drive you?

What do you notice yourself doing to avert those fears?

Do you find yourself sharing or holding the fears?

No way that you honestly answer will be wrong. It will just be what it is. The questions are a way to gather information to gain greater awareness and therefore greater access to oneself. Awareness offers empowerment. When we can see and understand ourselves better, we create a new lens for change. We become more mindful that a change or adjustment would work better. Awareness doesn't always give us the strength to take action on the change, but it does give us new eyes to see a higher road more clearly.

Sometimes, in the moment of the ask, we will not be able to locate an answer, and this is why: the question is planted consciously, but the answer will uproot from your subconscious mind, and that can take time. The subconscious mind is the true puppet master; it's the one running the whole show. We can't change anything in our lives if we don't know about it or have the awareness of it. It has to be brought forward to our awareness (conscious mind) so we can choose differently. When we know better, we do better, and the how always finds its way to us.

Over the years, fear changes its shape in the different phases of parenthood. Presently, I still hold the fear of losing Marley. I fear that

I won't finish my days here with her physically right next to me. I fear separation. I fear that if I did lose her, it would absolutely break me and I would never recover. I'm afraid of the intense pain it would cause me. I feel this mostly with Marley because her circumstances seem so fragile and unsure. I get a pit in my stomach and feel heaviness in my chest any time I think about it.

And now look, I'm hurting myself over and over again just by thinking about it! It hasn't happened and may never happen. So ***why do we do this***? We play out potential scenarios or circumstances. We *go there* for a moment in our minds. We feel the loss, the heartache, the fear. ***Why?*** It's the brain's way of trying to ***prepare*** us for mental distress. It's the heart's way of shielding us from emotional distress. Amazing and a little disturbing, right? Survival and self-preservation at their finest.

"I'm glad I felt so much of this earlier because it doesn't hurt so bad now," said no one ever.

I can let my fears drive all of my actions and efforts in keeping my children safe. And for years, I did. It still creeps in at times. Fear has a way of doing that, but overall I choose now to approach this same topic moved by the energy of love.

"Use the energy you have to believe, not to be afraid." —Unknown

I can exert my energy on worry and control. I can use it to make sure my children barely leave my sight. I can use it to keep them in a safe bubble, cutting them off from everything in the outside world. To me, none of this is sustainable. At some point, they will break or I will! Alternatively, I can use my energy to call in protection and guidance. I can use my energy to connect with my own intuition to know which people that come into our life are a yes or a no, and then I can take *that* a step further and act on it! I can use my energy to teach my children about safety and being aware of their surroundings. I can teach them to listen to their bodies, to notice the sensations they feel when they are around different people or in particular places. I can use my energy to help them find and use their voices and speak up for themselves. I can talk to them about my views around healthy sexuality and mutual consent. This alternative for me is a much more abundant investment.

Moving forward, with any choice you make for yourself and your family, ask yourself this: What is driving this choice: fear or love?

As a mother or parent, what are your fears for your child/children?

List your fears and then ask yourself: *why do these things scare me? Is it really about them or is it more about me?*

This chapter likely started to pull up some big feelings for you, and rightfully so. Empowerment comes when we learn how to properly manage this power we hold: ***emotions***. A part of us will want to run away, and that is OK. Just take notice of that desire. We have an override button available to us at any given moment. It is called ***the breath***. Take a few quiet moments and let me walk you through this guided meditation.

Mindfully start to connect to your breath. Intentionally inhale and exhale for five full rounds of breath, nice and slow. Lengthen your inhales and exhales as much as you can.

Notice the internal shifts within you as you communicate with your body through your breath. The breath is a language the body understands. The heart slows its rapid beating. The mind feels more quiet. The palms are not so sweaty. A sense of calm washes over you.

Continue with this breathing pattern and imagine yourself standing nice and tall. Your shoulders pull back and your sternum presses forward. Your feet are planted firmly on the ground with roots connecting you to your place and purpose here, to that one spot meant just for you. Breathe in, breathe out. The electrical energy and ancient wisdom of the earth shoot back up your feet, recharging every part of you like a battery.

You lift your face upward toward the sky, close your eyes, and feel the gentle sun bathe you in its warm light from the crown of the head to the tips of your toes. Arms at your sides, you let the shackles fall off of you as you turn your palms forward. Breathe in, breathe out. You feel lighter; more space and air move within you. You didn't know you could feel so weightless.

The light washes through you again. It is warm and rich and nourishes every part of you. All of the parts get equal portions of this light, even and especially the parts you don't feel are worthy of receiving it. Place your hand over your heart. The light fills in all the slices your heart holds. It feels like a warm hug. What would peace feel like in this moment? Breathe it in. What would self-acceptance feel like in this moment? Breathe it in. What would unconditional love for self and all the times you've picked yourself back up feel like in this moment? Breathe it in. Breathe all of this beauty in. Stay here, actively breathing for as long as you need to. You notice, through this experience, that some places or parts of you are bound. Maybe you hadn't realized how much. You can't unlock the chains if you don't know they're there.

CHAMBER 2

Rejection & Abandonment

"There are wounds that never show on the body that are deeper and more hurtful than anything that bleeds."

—Laurell K. Hamilton, *Mistral's Kiss*

The beliefs we carry about ourselves hold a point of origin. Beliefs are formed from the same thoughts we think over and over again. If we had multiple experiences and memories from childhood with not having parental support—physically, mentally, or emotionally—at times we really needed it, the thought arises, *I am alone and have to do everything on my own.* After looping this same thought over and over, it becomes a belief. The belief isn't necessarily true, but it *feels very true to us*. Here we find the term "my truth."

Rejection and abandonment are two core wounds. They are hurts that nearly everyone is familiar with from their individual experiences. The imprints left early on are deep, and with each additional experience of rejection or abandonment, the groove of the wound gets deeper and deeper and feels even more true.

Rejection: For most of my life, I felt rejected by my mother. She did not know how to mother me in the way that I needed. I was wired so differently from her. I didn't ever feel ***enough*** for her to love me the way I believed love to be. I didn't feel smart enough, kind enough, clean enough, obedient enough, or thoughtful enough. Through my little girl lens, I didn't have value worth loving. The attention I received most from her was critical and negative. Early on, I stopped trying to please her. I did not feel seen, heard, or validated in my feelings, nor safe to even share them. She never said, "I am sorry," at least not that I can remember. I hated discord. I didn't like how it felt, so when there were contentious feelings between us, I was always eventually the one to pull my shoulders back and bravely face her to apologize, just so things could feel a little better. The things I saw her focus on felt like they were more important than me. She never sat down. She was always doing housework and chores. There was always something that needed to be done. I didn't feel like I was worth her time or attention. I always felt like she was pushing me away, not physically but energetically. I didn't feel like she wanted to connect or ever spend time with me.

Then pile on years of all the things I wasn't chosen for or invited to: the friend's trip, the birthday party, the volleyball team, the lead role. The grooves of this core wound etched ever deeper with continued supporting evidence. Each experience adds weight to the groove. The wound is who you believe yourself to be: unlovable or not lovable enough, unworthy or unfitting in the eyes of others. *The evidence is all there*, we tell ourselves.

"The majority of suffering that we experience from our core wounds arises from the false self-image (or ego self) that we present to the world and try to protect. On the one hand, we go through life pretending to be very important, popular, 'together,' or acceptable. And on the other hand, we secretly believe that we are unworthy, ugly, unlovable, or broken deep down." —Aletheia Luna, lonerwolf.com/core-wound, "How To Find Your Core Wound (3 Practices)"

In what areas of your life and in what relationships do you feel rejected?

What have you made that mean about you?

What thoughts are you having about it (things you are telling yourself about it)?

Abandonment: When I was a young girl, my mom was in nursing school again. As a newlywed, she had almost completed her first year of school when she got a little surprise and found out she was pregnant with me. She dropped out of the nursing program not long after I was born. It was too stressful for her to do both school and take care of a newborn. As I got a little older, she went back and tried again, having to start the program from the very beginning. Not quite a year in, she got another surprise and was pregnant with my little brother! She dropped out again. It took her three tries to complete and be certified in one year of nursing school as an LPN. She finally completed it after my second little brother was old enough to be left with a sitter.

One morning, I asked her to help me curl my bangs. I had to go to school soon, and she was frantically trying to get herself out the door for her own school. She was running late and said she couldn't. I could see and feel her stress as she scrambled to get herself ready and out the door. I remember chasing after her, begging her, "Please, Mom! Just one curl! It will be so fast!"

Furrowing her eyebrows, she said again in an anxious tone, "I can't!" and she hurried out the door, slamming it shut. I chased after her, watching the car back out of our carport. She left me. I needed her, and she left me. I think it was raining that day. I remember the sky being dark and gloomy. I cried. I couldn't do it without her just yet. I didn't know how to work a hot curling iron by myself. I damn sure started practicing that day because I knew if I wanted it done, I had to do it myself. I couldn't count on her or anyone else to help me with this. The people I need always leave me. To a young child with a developing brain, this is how our belief systems are formed.

I have always felt alone, even in a crowded room. No one would guess that though, judging by the size of my friend group when I was growing up. I always felt different, and unsafe to be my truest self. I was always adapting to fit in with the crowd. I was a chameleon, a crowd follower. I never wanted to stand out. I tried to just blend in. *Please let me just fit in. Please only notice me for the positive.*

I always felt alone in my big feelings. I never felt like I fit in anywhere, though I tried desperately. That feeling of being alone continued with me into motherhood. I felt alone in making all the decisions for Marley. When I would talk to Josh or discuss what we should do regarding this or that for her, his answer was always the same: "Whatever you think." That was the evidence my brain needed to support this long-standing belief I held: *It's all up to me. If I don't do it, no one will. I have to do it myself.* The health and well-being of our daughter fell completely on my shoulders.

At the start of my personal healing work, this "alone" feeling showed up in a meditation. I felt it all everywhere in my body: the loneliness, the isolation, the disconnect, and the weight of it all. I saw a few scenes of my life flash in my mind like a movie. The first one was the operating room at the hospital the day I was born. I was taken out of my safe place via C-section and taken away from my mother. I was alone in a cold room with bright lights all around me. My arms and legs reached out in panic and fear. Everything was unfamiliar.

The next scene that flashed in my mind was in the family room of the first house I grew up in. I was a little toddler taking my first steps on our brown carpet. I'd tumble and fall and then pick myself back up and try again. No one was there to catch me. I was all alone.

In the last scene, I was a five-year-old girl carrying a heavy box. I didn't feel like I could share the contents of the box with anyone, so I carried the box alone. The box was full of secrets and the feelings tied to them.

These scenes reminded me of the loneliness, isolation, disconnect, and heaviness that were so familiar to me. And then, something unexpected happened during the meditation. The first scene in the hospital flashed again, but this time I could see what I couldn't see as a baby: The room was *filled* with people. It was standing room only. They were all Light Beings. It was my Divine Team. They were all there, so excited to witness my birth! "Look!" I could feel them say. "She is finally here. She is going to do big things!" I could feel their love and their excitement for me. I could feel their eagerness to support me in my new mission. I could see *now* something I couldn't see *then*: I wasn't really alone that day.

Then came the family room in the old house with the brown carpet where I took my first steps. The same Light Beings were all there again. They held their arms out, reaching to me as I tried toddling to them. They offered a hand to help me get up when I fell. "Look at her!" I could feel them say. "She is doing it!" Their faces looked like they had never witnessed a baby doing this before. They clapped their hands with excitement to see my progress. I could see now that I wasn't really alone that day.

Last was the five-year-old Karissa, trudging down the street with that heavy box. Her head hung low, but she didn't walk alone. The whole team was there again, walking right alongside her—alongside me. They placed their hands under the box so it didn't feel so heavy. They placed their arms around my shoulders to comfort me.

This beautiful experience illuminated the perspective I held for so long. The truth of each situation was that I was never really alone. It was a feeling, not a truth! I might not have felt human support in those exact moments, but there was most definitely always divine support. I still feel alone sometimes and that I am the only one I can depend on. When I am feeling this way, I turn to the memory of the insight I gained through that beautiful meditation. I pause and say to myself, *Karissa, remember, this is just an old feeling; it is not the truth of what is.* It automatically flips a switch inside of me. My mindset changes and so does my emotional state.

We want support, but often don't allow ourselves to see it or feel it when it is right in front of us! Such a paradox. We want to be validated, even if it hurts. We would rather be right than wrong.

See, we tell ourselves, I knew I was all alone. No one is ever there for me. I have to do everything on my own. The only person I can depend on is me. The brain wants to find continued evidence to support the running beliefs we hold about ourselves, others, and the world—again, in self-preservation.

Reflect on events in your own life. Does the alone feeling show up for you anywhere? Where?

Imagine yourself zooming out of your body and up into the stars, high above the earth. You have a whole new perspective that you didn't have before. Now ask yourself regarding each situation: What I am not seeing? Help me to see the truth of the situation.

With this new perspective, what do you see now that you couldn't see then, and how can you use this new information moving forward?

CHAMBER 3

Anger & Denial

One day, while I was emptying the dishwasher, I received a phone call. It was a friend from church. She'd called to tell me that she and her husband had been watching something on TV about autism. She stated, "We both think Marley has autism."

Her words cut me like a knife. I turned my gaze to the family room where my sweet little baby girl was playing on the floor with toys. I burst into tears, asking, "Why would you tell me that?" Her words felt like the meanest thing she could say to me!

From there, all I could see was red! I quickly hung up the phone and ran across the street to my mother-in-law's, hoping to get validation or confirmation that this friend's assessment was inaccurate. *Why did it anger me so much? Why did I feel like this friend was being so heartless? Why did it feel like an accusation? And why could I not even consider it?* I didn't want to consider for a minute that there could be truth in it. I couldn't handle it if it was true. She was totally wrong!

I asked two different therapists that came over weekly if they thought autism could be a possibility. Both of them said no. They said,

"She makes eye contact and responds to social cues. She doesn't have autism." That was sixteen years ago. The world has learned so much more about the autism spectrum since then. But back then, I dismissed the accusation and no one brought it back up for years.

Fast forward to Marley in preschool for early intervention at a local elementary school. I had three school-age kids at two different schools. Any mom of young kids knows what those mornings are like! One particular morning we were running behind, and I was scrambling to get everyone out the door. Overly tired, I had woken up late so I was in slippers and mismatched pajamas, and I was not wearing a bra as we hurried out the door for school. I knew how disheveled I looked. ***It's fine, I won't see anyone***, I thought. I dropped off the boys first then hurried to Marley's school. One perk of her being in special education was that I could pull into the kindergarten parking lot instead of going to the main school drop off. The kinder line was always shorter and faster. The paraprofessionals or her teacher would wait at the head of the line to greet the kids as they were dropped off. Then they would walk all the kids safely to class. That is, unless you are running late and they have already headed inside when you get there! I looked and felt like a hot mess, and on this day ***especially*** I was not about to park, unload Marley and Presley, walk Marley into the attendance office, sign her in, and walk her to class! Hard no. Presley was in her pajamas, buckled up in her carseat—a hot mess as well. I was not going in, no matter what!

I was determined to get Mar where she needed to be before that bell rang. After doing the first drop-off at one school, I pulled into the kindergarten parking lot and saw a long line. Of course, the other parents were scrambling to get their little ones to school on time too. I panicked! I looked to the head of the line for the paras and didn't see anyone. *They must have already gone in*! My panic escalated. I quickly scanned the little playground and could see her class was still out there. I thought if I could at least get her to the playground, the teachers could walk her to class. This was not going to be easy.

Marley was five, but she looked maybe three. She was tiny, shy, and unsure about everything. I knew she couldn't open the big heavy door of the car by herself or make her own way to the teachers halfway across the playground. I was desperate and did something that is the biggest no-no of school drop-off or pickup: I threw the car into park and got out! Braless and in slippers, I ran around to Marley's side and let her out. I couldn't—and didn't want to—get Presley out or go far from the car and leave her in there, so I tried to point to a colored object on the playground and told Marley to walk to it. She wouldn't move. She stopped dead in her tracks when she realized I wasn't going any further. She cemented her feet to the sidewalk and shook her head no! I heard honking from the car behind me, which only intensified the situation. *What was I going to do?* I was trying not to get frustrated with Marley, but I also needed her to move along. My voice was escalating.

I was a mix of nervous, embarrassed, anxious, fearful, angry, sad, frustrated, and annoyed. Just then the honking mother behind me threw her car into park and got out. She hollered to me, "Hey! You can't park here! I have a kid with special needs that I need to help get to class!"

I lost it! Without thinking, I yelled back, "Well, my kid has special needs and I have to help her get to class too!"

Marley's teacher finally saw my *running late* text and spotted Marley with her one foot on the playground. Despite the continual honking, I was not leaving that parking lot until I saw an adult with Marley's little hand in theirs. I was swallowed up in a tidal wave of emotions that overcame all reasoning. That fire had been quietly building inside of me for years! I felt the anger spewing out of me. I had been pricked by this woman's pin. I got back in my car and slammed the door closed behind me. My raging fire quickly melted into a puddle of hot tears.

The whole drive home I was filled with self-judgment for how I acted. Surely the other parents who witnessed this scene must have said, "That mom is crazy! Wow, that mom is really losing it!" I probably would have said the same thing.

What is it in us that doesn't mind witnessing this kind of spectacle? Is it that we can't relate? No, it's that we *can*. It's that for one moment we can look at another mother and feel better about ourselves. Instead of scooping her up in love and support, we relish in the fleeting lightness we feel as our own pain is lifted. We pat ourselves on the back instead of hugging her. I replayed all of it and then added my own narrative to the possible stories I was convinced they were telling themselves about me. I convinced myself they were true. How could they not be? I gave all the onlookers every evidence to support that I was nuts, and even worse, that I was a *bad mom*.

I had never said *special needs* about Marley out loud before. *Special needs* was so permanent. I was in total denial, a place I lived for years. It was the only way to get through it. I could not accept that special needs was even a possibility, so to me, it wasn't! Marley was just a little delayed, that was all. She'd catch up. *Did some part of me know? Why would I say that if I didn't believe it wasn't true?*

"Denial is a protective device, a shock absorber for the soul. It prevents us from acknowledging reality until we feel prepared to cope with that particular reality. People can shout and scream the truth at us, but we will not see or hear it until we are ready." —Melody Beattie, *The Language of Letting Go*

Denial is self-preservation. There it is again: we deny aspects of our circumstances because of the fear of what they may hold for us. I was angry this was our life, angry that everyone around us never could and probably never would understand how hard it is. *It makes me feel invalidated. They have no idea.* I was a ball of anger. I tried to keep anger at bay, but little bouts of that built-up energy would leak out sometimes. It would quickly turn into guilt and shame, and I'd feel lower than the dust of the earth. *Why am I so angry?*

Ask yourself:

> *What circumstances or events in my life is some part of me unwilling to accept?*
>
> *What am I hoping is not true? Is there something I am pretending not to see?*
>
> *What would it mean for me and for my family if it were true?*

In 2015, while seeking answers and remedies after my emergency surgery, out of desperation I turned to holistics. I had heard of a gifted woman in our state that was some kind of miracle worker. She was able to intuitively know where physical imbalances were in the body and what herbs to use for healing. I'd heard dozens of success stories from people that had gone to her. Some stories were as powerful as women finally being able to conceive a child after following her particular herbal regimen. I thought it was worth a try. After months of going for myself, I finally took Marley. Maybe this woman could find what was going on to help Marley get on track developmentally.

One day, I loaded up all four kids and drove thirty minutes for our appointment with this *witch doctor*—a name she was often jokingly called. It was a typical Arizona summer and the heat only magnified the chaos of juggling four kids at this follow-up appointment for Marley. Hazel the witch doctor did her usual mild prodding and poking, asking Marley and me questions. On her pink-lined paper, Hazel wrote down a different concoction of herbs for us to try for the next two months. Then she put her pen down, looked at me, and spoke in a softened tone.

"You know," she said as she fumbled with the Band-Aid that was wrapped around her finger, "I think Marley is perfect just the way she is." She paused and then continued, "I don't even think she needs to be baptized."

I felt a surge of emotions rise within me. I was so confused as I tried to process what she was saying. The only reaction I remember having was tears. Even though I didn't understand them, her words broke my heart. I must have felt something in her tone. *Did she mean Marley was going to die young? Before the eight-year-old age of baptism in our church?* Is that what she meant? My mind was swirling, trying to understand what she was hinting at. I gathered up my kids, along with my shattered heart, and left. Once in the safe space of my car, I called Josh and unleashed over the nerve of this woman! I tore her to shreds. I used every profanity in the book. Josh was shocked. I never spoke like this! I was just as shocked.

Hazel the witch doctor *knew*. She *knew* Marley's delays in development could not be remedied with an herbal tincture. She tried to gently tell me that, but I wouldn't hear it. Instead, I dismissed her as crazy and harsh. She became my punching bag and was immediately discredited. *Who was she to tell me this? What was she even trying to say?* I was done with her, and I never went back. Half-empty bottles of liquid herbs sat on my shelf for years after that. *What did she know anyway?*

CHAMBER 4

Jealousy & Resentment

On the first day of school in Marley's second year of being in the self-contained classroom, I looked around to scan the faces. There was one little face I did not see. Concerned, I asked the teacher, "Where is Nathan?"

She replied, "He moved over to Gen Ed."

Stunned, I looked at her and didn't say a word back. My heart sank. *Why could that child move over and not mine?* His symptoms had seemed more severe than Marley's. I couldn't believe it! Marley followed directions and completed tasks. The teachers never had a hard time managing her. It blew my mind that this little boy was able to be mainstreamed now.

I saw his mother later that day and asked her about it.

"We put him on medication for ADHD and it made all the difference!" *Medication? That was all it took for him?* These two little friends had been in class together since early intervention preschool. I felt left behind and stuck. I was embarrassed that Marley was in the self-contained class. I resented that this was where she "belonged." I did not want her to be labeled like that. She was higher functioning than most of the students there but not high enough to be mainstreamed, even with the support of a paraprofessional. *Nathan went on and left us*, I thought, *and we are still here . . . still in the same place. This feels so unfair.*

After my third consecutive miscarriage, I was done trying. I was done continually getting my heart broken. To be honest, I was done seeing pregnant people, done hearing about baby showers, done hearing that so-in-so just found out what gender her baby was. I was *done.* At the same time, though, it didn't feel final. I decided to try one more time to stay pregnant and that would be it. I couldn't even trust the pink plus sign when it popped up in the test window. I didn't want to get my hopes up.

I'll never forget the feeling I had when I saw a cluster of pink balloons move past my dining room window. I knew who they were for, and it wasn't for me. They were for my neighbor. She was pregnant and had never known miscarriage. All of her children were healthy and neurotypical. The sign of pink told me she had found out she was having a girl. I sobbed. Of course it worked out for her. Of course she was having a girl. It wasn't that I didn't want that for her, I just couldn't understand why things always worked out for her and not me. My old pain wrapped around my heart like the string from one of those damn pink balloons.

I was jealous and resentful of her advantages. It wasn't singular to her—there were others too. Were these others really that much better than me that things in life just always went their way? I wondered if *I* could be the factor. Maybe I wasn't good enough. But how could that be? I was literally doing all the things I had ever been taught by religion, family, and society to establish a "good," close, obedient, God-fearing family. I followed all the "rules." I did everything one must to receive "blessings" from God and to be worthy of miracles. I wondered, *who in the hell is doing more than me*? It seemed impossible! Maybe they were reading scriptures longer than I was? Maybe that was it? Maybe I was too inconsistent with our family on Saturdays. What was I doing wrong? What was I missing? Surely everyone has to experience hard things in life, but why did it seem like some people's hard didn't even compare to mine?

There was nothing I could do with these feelings. What *would* I even do? I couldn't own them or claim them, even within myself. The thought made me feel two feet tall. It was incriminating and shameful. I didn't dare do it. Maybe if I never claimed them, they weren't really there.

I had always fallen in line and done what I was told. I never got into any real trouble as a teen and never questioned authority or leadership, aside from my parents. I never took counsel through my own filters. I was not secure enough in myself and in my connection to God to trust my own answers. I believed the higher ups always knew better than me.

When Marley was almost eleven, I knew the next round of standard immunizations was coming up. Since I had started to see myself and Marley differently, I started seeing everything differently! The school had asked me about proof of immunizations and I said I wasn't sure about doing them yet. Prior to this point, I had immunized all of my children. This was the first time in sixteen years of being a mother that I actually asked myself, *Am I going to immunize? Is this really the right thing for Marley?* This was the first time I gave myself permission to even ask a question like this.

When she was young and showing developmental delays, I had asked our pediatrician about side effects of vaccines and the hearsay link to autism. He would say, "There have been no studies to prove that there is any direct correlation." That had always been enough for me. This person was a professional. He knew more than me. He was also a trusted family friend. Why would I question him or think I knew more? I never questioned, I fell in line, and I immunized all of my children. Mind you, I was asking these questions sixteen years ago. So much in the way we are able to access information has changed since then.

I started doing my own research. Ashamedly, I honestly had never done that before on any subject. I didn't have space in me for research or what I might find. It was too overwhelming. When I finally did do research, I didn't like what I was finding. I couldn't believe how much I didn't know. I couldn't believe how much I had trusted someone else's authority over my own. I prayed. I felt into it. I gathered all the information about immunizations—the positives and the negatives. I sat with it for a while. Marley's eleventh year was nearly ending and still, I sat with this decision. The more I sat with it, the worse I felt about doing it. The more I leaned toward *not* doing it, the more peace I felt!

I still hadn't made a concrete decision. It felt so weight-bearing to declare a definitive choice. I had to go with my gut and ask myself what felt right to me. I had never allowed myself to do that before. I had been programmed since infancy that all the answers I needed in life were outside of me—God, Jesus, Holy Spirit, and ecclesiastical leaders were all outside of me. There were also teachers, coaches, guides, doctors, and administrative leaders—again, all outside of me. *Why would I ever look in if I had always been taught to look out?*

Up until this time, I had no reason to ask questions. I had no reason to quest for different results. There was no agitation or friction to propel me to seek something different—no catalyst, no reason to question the system. It worked for me for a long time. Marley was my catalyst. She made me look at things and ask questions that I never had to before. I knew the doctor and I know that he honestly believed what he told me. The system was working for him personally and with the majority of his patients. I didn't know what was causing Marley's neuro differences, but I did know that continuing to immunize would not benefit her, and that was a risk I was not willing to take. My knowing spoke, and I chose to listen.

During this time, I was talking with a friend. I was sharing this conundrum, the back-and-forth, push-and-pull of this decision. When I asked what she would do, she quickly said, "I've always just done it. It's easier that way."

My heart started racing and I instantly reacted, firing back, "If you had a daughter like Marley, you would put more thought into it." It stung to hear her say what she had said, but it stung even more that I snipped at her and spoke to her that way. I was hurting and it came out in a way that had nothing to do with her. Her kids were *normal.* They were healthy and right on track developmentally. It wasn't her fault. She had no reason to question the system. It was working for her.

It is hard to say the right thing to a mother, especially when she is hurting. One day, a woman relayed to me something that happened with her son and Marley. Marley had taken a toy that belonged to this boy and wouldn't give it back. He was mad and frustrated with her but told his mom that he couldn't stay mad at her because, "It's Marley." She continued to tell me, "We talked about it and I just said to him, 'Aren't we so lucky to have Marley to help us learn these things?'"

I know she meant well. I stood there fuming underneath my half smile. *How did she not get it?* This is what I *heard*: "I am so glad you could have a daughter with special needs so my normal child can learn how to love and quickly forgive."

I am so glad I could do that for you—take one for the team like that, I thought.

Her comment stung for a while. I wished that for one day she could be in my shoes and know what this felt like. She would never know. No one in my family could either. You can't know it if you haven't lived it. Attempts for empathy often get expressed as sympathy. I didn't need anyone to feel sorry for me. I just wanted people to *really* come down to my level—to meet me where I was and *try* to see through my lens. What I wanted wasn't even humanly possible. It was unfair of me to hold others to a standard of understanding they could never reach, but I did it anyway.

I came across an old journal entry of mine that read: "I'm angry and sad. I'm annoyed that everything works out so perfectly for the same people."

The year I wrote it is irrelevant because it could have applied to a number of years of my life. This feeling was so much deeper than annoyed, angry, or sad. Those are all acceptable human feelings. They seem normal to claim and easy to validate. But jealous? Women my age were not supposed to be jealous anymore. We are supposed to be past that, bigger than that. Jealousy is an immature, childlike, teen-phase feeling. *What would that say about me, a grown woman, admitting feelings of jealousy?*

To feel wholeness and acceptance for your circumstances, you must find acceptance for yourself first. That comes with owning all the parts of you, even the ones you hide or pretend aren't there. You may not be able to vocalize them, but these feelings want to be seen and acknowledged. That is why they are there. Emotions are the internal messages that some part of us is seeking love, recognition, and thoughtful attention.

Ask yourself:

Where do I feel jealousy and/or resentment in my life? Is it toward a person? A circumstance or event?

Who do I most often project my own hurt onto?

Where do I feel jealousy and resentment in my body?

What have I made having these feelings mean about me?

If you are unsure how to find the place where this emotion lives in your body, close your eyes and tap into those feelings. Reflect on the people or circumstances that cause you to feel those painful emotions. You will find the place in your body. It might be some kind of sensation, ache, or dull pain. It could be in your heart space, shoulder, neck, belly, or back. Pay attention to what's happening inside your body. Once you locate the place, say, "I see you, jealousy. I see you, resentment. I know you are there because I am hurting. Thank you for showing me a part of me that needs more love and attention." Take three deep breaths in and out, mindfully breathing into that wounded place. Take notice of a color, texture, or image that may come to mind in that area.

Journal about what you noticed, what you experienced, and any other insight or clarity you gained.

Ask yourself, *what do I do with this now?* Trust that your higher self will guide you to your next step.

CHAMBER 5

Regret

I raised all of my babies in the same house for nearly nineteen years. It was all they ever knew. When we moved, we didn't go far. It was just next door, actually! Even though our new home felt airy and light, fresh and new, I was having a hard time saying goodbye to our old house. It made it a little easier to know that the new owners loved it and were happy there.

One day, I couldn't pinpoint what I was feeling, but I knew I didn't like it. I decided to journal all the thoughts I was having and use them like bread crumbs to find the root.

This is from that journal entry:

How do you really say goodbye? How do you let go of something that had so much purpose and meaning to you?

Two decades worth of our memories are held there. The house helped keep them alive because there were constant physical reminders at every turn.

This is the room where I rocked all of my babies to sleep and kissed them goodnight.

This is the kitchen where we made cookies. The kids' soft little hands with dimples still in them, patting and pressing the dough.

This is the table where the kids did homework, and we ate meals together as a family.

This is the stairway where the kids lined up their mattresses and slid down them, bouncing and laughing the whole way down.

This is the fireplace where we read Christmas stories together and drank hot cocoa.

This is the closet where Marley first wrote her little name on the wall. (It was such a typical thing for my non-typical child to do. I never cleaned it off, I loved it so much.)

This is where the boys played football interceptions with their dad, laughing and jumping up and down.

This is the basketball court where we could hear Drey bouncing the ball for hours at night.

This is the pantry where Crew dumped out ALL of the flour when he was little.

This is the door frame that little Drey wrapped his arms around when we got home from being out of town.

This is the closet where little Presley loved to dress up in all my fancy shoes—boots up to her knees!

This is where we sang songs together and played chase.

This whole house holds our whole life!

I am afraid that if I let the house go, I will lose all the memories with it. I don't want to lose the memories of their childhood. Will I forget all the tender moments? Will I forget all the laughter? I want to hold onto the happiness, tenderness, and laughter even among all the struggle and pain. I don't really know what I am feeling, but it's something I don't want to let go of.

Then, just like that, I found it. *I wanted to go back!* It really wasn't about the house. The house was mirroring a deeper feeling I held. I was feeling the pain of regret! Does anyone know the feeling of regret better than a mother?

I wish I could go back. I wish I knew then the things I know now. I wish I would've been more present. The energy of regret is always past. When we hold on to regret, we are bringing past pain to the present. A part of me would love to go back and parent my kids as the current version of me, but we are not meant to go back. Regret keeps us in a stagnant energy. We cannot change what was, we can only learn from it and do differently moving forward, if that is what we choose. This is where we alchemize regret and use it as a teacher, applying yesterday's lessons today.

What regret do you carry?

How is carrying this regret serving you? Why do you think you are holding on to it?

Is it possible to shift your lens on that situation or circumstance? What would that feel like?

How can you alchemize what you've learned since then and do differently moving forward?

CHAMBER 6

Guilt & Shame

Guilt is the ideal breeding ground for shame. Guilt is "I did." Shame is "I am." I *did* let her get out of my sight and into the road where she was nearly hit by oncoming traffic, therefore, I *am* a terrible mother. They go hand in hand. The guilt fed my shame and the shame fed my unworthiness. I wasn't worthy to have Marley for a daughter. I was entrusted with her care and I was failing. I didn't deserve such a special soul. I didn't deserve the title of *mother*.

We were at the end-of-the-season party for the boys' flag football team in our neighbor's backyard. As I sat nursing Presley, I allowed myself to catch up with a friend I hadn't seen in a while. This moment of reconnecting came to a quick halt when I heard a woman holler over the fence, "Hey! There is a little girl on the main road!"

Fear and adrenaline shot through my body, propelling me out of my seat. I knew it was Marley! I handed Presely over and sprinted down the driveway and all the way out to the main road. Fear and panic surged through my veins. *Oh my God, what was I going to find?* Sure enough, there she was at the edge of the street: my tiny girl with her hair in two top knots was sitting on a red wiggle car. She was completely unaware of the danger. As I approached the scene, two women who had parked their car and gotten out, certainly afraid for this little girl, asked me, "Are you her mother?"

"Yes," I answered solemnly.

They continued, "And you let her ride into the street?" I didn't answer. They started speaking to each other in Spanish. Unbeknownst to them, I understood every word.

"What kind of mother lets this happen?" they asked each other. "She wasn't even watching her," they continued.

They were right. Here was more evidence to validate the heavy feelings I already carried. What kind of mother allows herself to take her gaze off of this little girl? Clearly, one that is unfit. I picked Marley up and started dragging the wiggle car behind me as we headed back home. One of the women said, "You can't leave! We've called the police and they are on their way. They will want to talk to you!"

I turned around and said, "If they want to talk to me, they can come find me."

I flipped back around and walked home, tears burning the brave face I had just put on. *Is this really happening? And now the police are coming? Could they take away my daughter? Am I really so unfit?* I already knew the answer to that question: of course I was.

The police did come and they found me before Marley, the wiggle car, and I made it home. There were a lot of questions and a lot of tears. The officer was kind and just doing his job. He had every right to wonder if this child really was safe. I told my version of what happened, told him that my daughter was delayed and had no concept of danger. I told him she is so hard to keep in sight and that these gates are almost always closed. It was a total fluke accident that both the gate to the backyard and the gate to the neighborhood were wide open. I can't remember if he asked for my name or for Marley's. All I remember was the fear I felt and the heavy shame and guilt I carried.

The officer ended the conversation with, "If this happens again, we will have to file a report."

I nodded my head and carried my baby home. *I can't do this,* I thought to myself, the way I had nearly every day of her entire life. It was such a familiar statement. It was such a familiar feeling. *What kind of mother lets this happen?* It swirled around and around in my mind.

In the world of personal development, shadow work is a concept first introduced by Carl Jung. My understanding is that one's shadow consists of the parts of us we keep hidden—that we don't want to show—and that we even pretend are not there. Once we bring something out of hiding and into light (into the open), it is no longer hidden. It is no longer a shadow. In my case, I was pretending that I didn't hold such negative feelings about Marley's circumstances. I never showed, spoke about, or acknowledged them to anyone—not my husband or even within myself.

The antidote for shame, or any kind of shadow, is light. It is doing the opposite of what you naturally want to do to feel safe: shine a spotlight on that which you would prefer to keep hidden. I didn't dare admit how much internal friction I harbored. The shame buried underneath it all made me want to crawl into a hole and never come out. Integrating the shadow of shame does not mean abolishing shame. It is the acknowledgement that this feeling has a place in you.

So many parts of this book were once my shadows, which I brought into the light. I once pushed these parts away from me. I couldn't claim them because, *what would that say about me* if I did? I finally chose to pull these parts in closer and get really honest about all of them. I realized it was never about Marley, it was about me. I rejected an aspect of my life because I rejected so many aspects of myself.

CHAMBER 7

Judgment

The facial expression I saw on the women that called the police is one I have seen many times from other concerned parents.

"Were you even watching her?" a family member asked, his face full of fear and tears as he knocked on our front door to bring Marley back to us. She had been playing in the backyard, somehow gotten out, and was toddling her way toward the big white gates at the end of our street.

Maybe these faces full of judgment thought they could do better? In those moments, I probably would have agreed with them. I was not cut out for this. I was not capable enough. *Why me? Why was this burden placed on me? Why was I asked to do this?* It was too hard, and clearly I was failing desperately at my daughter's expense. *Just chain me up and drop me to the bottom of the sea. That is where I belong.* Sometimes I had these thoughts when I saw the looks on others' faces. There were also other times when their comments fueled my fire and I thought, *if you think you can do better, I'd like to see you try!*

Recently, Marley screamed "bitch hole" twice at my friend's son's birthday party. I was there without Josh, so I was already feeling alone.

Our whole neighborhood was there, along with all of our family. My mother-in-law gasped—literally putting her hand to her chest—she was so horrified. I don't why because this isn't a new thing for Marley. Marley was losing it, her veins popping out on her neck. I tried to ignore the first "bitch hole" and not feed it with any attention. I couldn't ignore the second one and instantly snapped. I marched right over to Marley and tried reaching for her arm but caught hold of her shoulder. "Ouch! You're hurting me!" she yelled. *Great, that's all I need!*

It doesn't bother me when she swears because I know she doesn't even understand what she is saying. They are just words. They don't have meaning other than what we have assigned to them. It only bothers me when I start to care what *other people* are thinking and how they must be viewing Marley and me. I'm sure they are thinking, *Why doesn't she do something? That is such terrible behavior. Marley is too old to be talking like that, especially in public! My child would never do that!*

When I am wrapped up in myself and am hypersensitive to the perceptions of others, I naturally start telling myself all the things *they must be saying.* Sometimes I feel invincible, secure, and confident, like nothing can stick to me. Other times I feel fragile, quiet, and withdrawn. This is how I felt walking into the party. This is why I felt alone in a room full of people I knew. This is why the whole thing stuck to me so much.

We feed our emotions when we bring in more of the same thoughts. In a matter of seconds, we spiral deeper and deeper down the emotional scale. The judgment I feel quickly turns to guilt and always ends with shame. When I reach shame, there isn't much lower I can go. *Chain me up, and drop me to the bottom of the sea.* I didn't start there, but one thought quickly feeding the other is how I arrive at those depths.

I feel judgment for how she talks, dresses, and laughs. I feel judgment for her mannerisms, hand gestures, and facial expressions. Everyone is judging her in some way, which feels like a judgment of me. It stings. Really, the question is, am I secure enough in myself that I can be OK with whatever their thoughts are about Marley? About me? That is where our work is. It is always about us, not them. ***Always.***

"What sense does Marley have?" a boy recently asked when he was over playing one day. I knew exactly what he was trying to say, but I stubbornly made him find more words.

"What do you mean?" I asked.

He continued, "Why does she make a funny laugh and hide under the table sometimes?"

"I know, she is so funny, right?" I wouldn't let up.

"Like, what sense does she have? Like, why is she so weird?" He continued to try to find more words.

I felt my heart beat a little faster. I paused for a moment and took a deep breath, restraining myself from letting this eight-year-old have it. "Her brain just works differently than everyone else's."

I didn't know what to say to help him or the other kids understand Marley better. What I felt in his ask was judgment and differentness. The kids around us were all at least six years younger than her, and they *still* noticed that she was different—weird even. No mother wants to hear that, even when she knows it. The win for me was that his words didn't burn as bad as when I heard them like they have so many times before. The words almost always stung, even if it was a little kid saying them. My heartstrings strummed for a couple hours after this exchange.

"What should I have said? What would you have said?" I later asked Josh. "What would an eight-year-old understand? Should I have said autism?"

"Maybe so," he said. "That is a term I think a lot of kids these days have heard."

It isn't an easy explanation. Many adults don't really understand either and often act surprised by her behavior. Does this mean he doesn't want to play with her? Or was he just making an observation? I can't control him or any other kid. All I can really do is hope the comment comes from curiosity, not judgment. Can I let his comment be neutral?

Marley is so cool, quirky and fun! That is what I want people to notice and observe. That is how I want people to see her, but I can't control the lens through which they are looking. Can I be OK with that? Sometimes I can, and sometimes it is so hard!

Where do you feel the most judgment in your life? Can you think of specific examples or memories?

Are there certain people or groups that you feel the most judgment from?

Where do you hold the most judgment for yourself?

What would it feel like if you could free yourself from the judgment of others?

CHAMBER 8

Grief

For all of the years I spent trying to figure out Marley, someone I loved and respected planted the seed that she might have a genetic disorder—maybe Down syndrome. I had never considered it. What I knew of it didn't seem to match her. I opened my mind to the possibility. As I explored it, I found something called Mosaic Down syndrome. As I read about it, I was surprised how many of the symptoms she had! I thought about it and quietly sat with it. I shared it with Josh. For over a decade we had not found a diagnosis for Marley, and because there was nothing concrete, I always thought it was something I was supposed to find and fix. There was no hard evidence to support that she "had" something, but what if she did? Was this the puzzle piece we were missing all this time? *Could Marley have a genetic disorder?*

Part of me thought it made so much sense! I had internal bells going off all over the place. The other part of me processed what this would mean. It felt like a scarlet letter she would never be rid of. No one would want to take her to prom. No one would want to date or marry her. She *couldn't* marry. This would follow her forever.

The life I imagined for my daughter took a hard turn that I was not ready for. There was some kind of knowing in my body that I couldn't explain. It seemed like information I knew somewhere inside of me was now coming forward. Grief is the crushing feeling of despair: deeply feeling the loss of what will never be.

I grieved that there would be no prom dates. I grieved the loss of a dad walking his precious daughter down the wedding aisle. I grieved the loss of a white picket fence and olive-skinned grandchildren with green eyes just like their mama. I grieved that womanhood would look so much different on Marley. I grieved the loss of the mother-daughter relationship I had once pictured. I grieved the loss of loving and connecting with her the way I wanted to.

In the dark early hours one morning, as the busy world still slept, I sat alone in my closet. My mind and heart were racing, processing this new potential reality of a genetic disorder. As I sat there hugging my knees into my chest, wallowing in a sea of swirling thoughts, I lost it. I cried, moaned, and wailed in a way I never had before. *What did this mean?* I thought. *What will our life look like? What do I do?*

Moments later Josh walked in, hugged me, and said, "It's OK. If she does have it, it doesn't change anything. It's not a big deal."

I felt my deep sadness and despair instantly liquify into boiling hot lava. In my rage, I pushed him away as I yelled, "*To you*, Josh! It's not a big deal *to you*!" I screamed at the husband who had just minimized my feelings, "Just let me cry! Let me scream! Let me agonize! Let me pity myself! Let me curse God! Let me grieve and mourn a life that will never be! Let me just feel all of my feelings without making me feel wrong for having them! That's great that *you* are OK, but I am allowed to have a moment where I am not OK!" He was stunned and didn't know how to respond. As he silently turned to walk away, I knew I had crushed him. Now we were both crushed.

The next few months were heavy and hard. I was in deep grief, processing how different our life would be. The reality I presently knew and futuristically hoped for would be completely different. Grieving, and *allowing* oneself to grieve, is an essential part of the healing process. I gave myself the gift of embracing my emotions without judgment. I knew these emotions wouldn't stay with me forever. I knew they would move because, really, that is their purpose: the movement of energy. I knew they needed to be recognized, acknowledged, *felt!*

Sometimes I feel a twinge of grief when I think about the kids growing up, moving out, and having their own lives. I wonder if Marley will ever think, *what about me?* Will she be content to stay? Will she be sad or lonely not having them home? The way she knew life to be in her formative years will not be that way forever. Will she even understand why those she loves are leaving her?

Sometimes, I feel a twinge of grief when Presley is out with her friends on a Friday night and Marley is home with Mom and Dad. Sometimes, I wish Marley had a bunch of friends she liked to hang out with and felt comfortable with, friends that knew her and understood her. But Marley is Marley. Sometimes what I want for her is not what she really wants. There have been many times I've tried to get her together with friends and she still just sticks to herself. I have since accepted that Marley's life, our life, will look different. I mostly feel peace, but sometimes sadness still swirls in. Letting go has ebbs and flows.

Every time I read through this chapter throughout the many phases of writing and editing, my eyes fill with tears. Grief isn't a onetime event or process. It isn't something that can be checked off the to-do list of healing, and true healing is not the absence of grief. In the thick of our grieving, we don't feel like we will ever be OK or go on with life as it is. We know we are healing when the ache and despair for what will never be doesn't feel as sharp or as deep, and when we know from somewhere deep within us that we can and will keep going.

What aspect of your life are you currently grieving?

Is there a dream or future vision that has not come to fruition?

Is it within a relationship?

How do you deal with grieving what you hoped for?

Do you need permission to grieve? If so, what would that look like?

Using the tools you learned in a previous chapter, find where you hold that grief in your body. Journal what you discover.

PART 3

REMEDY & REPAIRING

CHAPTER 7

Repairing the Inner Child

The first time I went to therapy was by accident, really. I was there with a close friend who was clearly a mess. She asked me to sit in with her. Stacy had been an addict for years. She struggled with depression and a constant stream of health problems. She never really could get on top of it all. We'd often have conversations about her getting back up on the horse when she got kicked off, only to find her days or weeks later having been "kicked off" again. Stacy and I were really no different. She turned to numbing agents, I put on a mask and played a part. Both of us had deep wounds that we coped with so differently. She never tried to camouflage her pain, and I tried to push through mine the only way I knew how. I didn't feel I had permission to be sad, hurt, or angry.

At Stacy's appointment—that I was sitting in on—Glenda, the practitioner, explained to us her methods. She was a hypnotherapist, Reiki master teacher, who also developed her own eye movement stress release process. I didn't know what any of that meant. She explained how she clears old, trapped emotions, allowing one to experience greater peace and wholeness by getting in alignment with their true self. I hung on her every word. She spoke about the soul and its agreements before coming to earth. Tears rolled down my cheeks. I had never heard anything like this before, and yet it felt so familiar to me. My soul recognized truth in the things she spoke.

Stacy looked at me, puzzled about why I was crying at *her* appointment! I thought I had been led to this therapist for Stacy, but it was for me. Glenda observed my tears, turned to me, and said, "I have a cancellation right after this appointment if you want to go next?" I nodded my head in complete agreement. One hour with Glenda lifted one hundred pounds of weight off my back. I could not believe how light I felt! How was this possible? I didn't quite understand what she did or how it worked, but the proof was in how I felt. I'd *never* felt this way!

Two weeks prior, I lay in my bed sobbing in defeat and despair. The year was 2015. I had the emergency surgery in April and by fall I did not feel any better and in some regards worse! The brain fog was unreal. I was in physical, spiritual, mental, and emotional anguish. I couldn't tell up from down—I didn't know what I needed. For months, I felt at the mercy of my circumstances, when finally one day, I firmly pleaded with God. "This will not be my forever! You *have* to show me the things that will help me heal!"

Now, here I was sitting with a woman I had just met, doing a healing process I had never heard of! I was desperate and by divine synchronicity led to the person who could help me. Using all of her modalities, Glenda helped me release years of trapped emotions I was carrying and unable to fully process until now. Trapped trauma and any issue that causes stress releases at a cellular level, and the body and mind can be retrained to respond differently.

I couldn't understand why my childhood hurts had such a strong hold on me. They still felt so fresh. I often beat myself up for not being able to just get over them. It was in Glenda's cozy brown chair that I first learned about the inner child. We grow out of childhood thoughts and beliefs, *right?* Honestly, *no.* We keep those same running beliefs about ourselves—the thoughts and patterns of behavior—until we gain awareness of how much they are still running us as adults. The inner child holds the patterns, and we can't change them if we don't know what they are. For the very first time in thirty-three years, I dove headfirst into the exact place I had always tried to wall off. It was such a foreign concept, the idea of running *toward* the pain rather than away from it. Was the process hard? *Yes.* Did I cry? *Yes.* I sobbed—over and over again. Was it worth it? *Absolutely.*

I went to Glenda consistently for years. I continued diving straight into the wounds. Some sessions were harder than others. My body knew I'd feel so much better afterward, which kept my mind from talking me out of going. Roots to the deep scars I carried became more and more illuminated. This awareness gave me understanding and compassion for myself—something I had never experienced before. More pieces of the puzzle came together. Over time, old memories came forward and asked that I look at them, and I did. I was surprised to learn that nothing was wrong with me! There were reasons I developed the thought patterns I had. There was a deeply wounded inner child aching for safety, security, and protection—a deeply wounded inner child who was feeling incredibly weak, small, powerless, and craving love without condition.

I was a mother—much older and a little bit taller—but those same beliefs I held about the world and myself when I was a child were *all* still there, still in effect!

Mirror Work: This is a practice developed by Louise Hay for the purpose of connecting to one's inner self. She writes about it in *Mirror Work: 21 days to Heal Your Life*. Look in the mirror, directly into your own eyes. Can you do it? What emotions swirl inside you as you attempt it? Any discomfort? The power of the mirror is that it honestly reflects back the feelings we have about ourselves. Hay encourages making this a daily practice and adding in positive affirmations. Over time we become less critical of ourselves as we change our self-talk while looking in the mirror.

The mirror concept also offers a deeper window into the self. We constantly project our own thoughts, feelings, and beliefs onto others. It wasn't Marley hurting, it was me. It wasn't Marley wanting to be accepted and loved, it was me. It wasn't Marley wanting to belong, it was me.

The relationship you have with yourself is the most important relationship you will ever have, and it spills onto every single person around you. If you can't love yourself, you cannot fully love another. If you can't accept yourself, you cannot fully accept another. If you are quick to judge yourself, you will easily judge others. When we change how we see ourselves, this new lens follows us everywhere. We start to see everything with new eyes. Your work is to lovingly mend your relationship with yourself. When you focus loving attention there, the pieces of your broken heart will slowly come back together. It is a process of patience, effort, and consistency, but one day you will feel differently. You will see differently. You will wake up in a place of peace and contentment for yourself, just as you are.

"How long must one wait in the dark? Until one learns to see in the dark." —Florence Scovel Shinn, ***The Game of Life and How to Play It***

Inner child work involves seeing those parts of yourself—witnessing and acknowledging the parts that experienced any kind of pain or sadness, great or small—and then giving yourself now what you didn't have then. The benefits of this work are life-changing, while the practice itself is actually quite simple.

I wanted a girl because, unknowingly, I wanted to mother little Karissa. I wanted to hug her, snuggle her, stroke her hair, hold her face in my hands and look deep into her eyes and tell her she was the most beautiful thing I ever created. The mirror in this is that those are all the things *I* always wanted to hear. I thought that by doing and saying all those things for my daughter, my hurts would be made right. But the solution was always for me to extend those things ***to myself***. I was so blinded by my own pain, I could not see that Marley was perfect just as she was. I spent years trying to change her when it was me who needed changing.

Can you allow yourself to finally look at your old hurts? It is time. It may seem overwhelming and you may say, "I don't even know where to start!" As my friend Julie Elizabeth once told me, "You start, sister, from the beginning. Go back to the little you. Teach her, love her, reparent her with the proper stewardship. In this, you will find radical acceptance."

Start mending the little you by honoring her needs. All of them.

Physical: Use the restroom when you need to; stop holding it. Nourish your body with food when it is asking for it. Allow yourself to rest when your body is asking for it. Look at taking care of you as though you are parenting the little you. If the little you needed to use the restroom, wouldn't you tell her to go? Or if she was hungry, wouldn't you feed her? Keep her (you) physically safe. Be mindful of where you allow yourself to go and with whom you surround yourself. Safety is a primal need and is often our earliest wounding. Pay attention to sensations in your body when you're with other people. Do you feel uneasiness in your belly? Do your palms get sweaty? Or does your body feel quiet and settled? Sensations are the language of the body. Take time to pause and listen to them.

Mental: Pay attention to your thoughts and words. Do not speak anything that you would not say to a young child. This includes quiet thoughts. If a younger you said, "I can't do that thing. I would never be good at it," would you say, "Yeah, you're right. Don't even try"? No, you wouldn't. Don't say it to yourself now either. "I am" are the two most powerful words we could ever string together. They are not just words, they are declarations. You are saying what is so. When you say, "I am so dumb," you are declaring it. "I am not good enough" is, again, a declaration. They are powerful statements. The same is true for things like, "I am strong. I am supported." Declarations. Statements. Truth. In this new practice of noticing, how many times in a day do you use the phrase *have to*? I *have* to do this or that. Do you really *have to*? There is an energetic weight connected to *have to*. Consider changing your verbiage to "I am choosing to" or "I get to." It feels different. Give it a try!

To start changing the language you use with yourself, develop a regular practice of positive affirmations. Set an alarm every day to help you remember. It may seem uncomfortable and unnatural at first. It may be a struggle to find the words. Over time, however, you will feel them as truth in every cell of your body. You are breathing in new life, restructuring the old, wounded operating systems that you have been running on your whole life. Eventually, positive words will come more naturally. You will start speaking them more freely. Over time, your tone will change as you speak them because you are slowly waking up to the truth of who you really are and what you are capable of.

Untangling is a practice of awareness. When you notice yourself saying something unkind to yourself, whether it is a quiet thought or vocalized words, pause and replace it with a kind statement about yourself. How would you feel if you heard your child speaking ill of themself? You are no less worthy of receiving the same treatment and respect. You are untangling the relationship you have with yourself, lovingly mending it so you can do the same process with your child. I noticed a shift within myself after starting this daily practice, so I naturally wanted to share it with my children. I would set the alarm as a reminder when we were in the car driving to school. I noticed a huge shift within Marley after a little while. I would say the affirmation and she would repeat it after me. The tone of her voice and her body language changed when she repeated the affirmations. She stood a little taller, pulling her shoulders back. She was starting to believe the truths she was speaking to herself. The same will happen for you.

Emotional: Practice saying "no" to commitments that do not serve you or do not truly benefit you. Establish boundaries with those you are not energetically aligned with, even if they are family. Avoiding people because they trigger you is not the same as setting boundaries, but maybe that is what it will look like in the beginning. Pay attention to feelings of obligation. In what places do you self-abandon? How does it serve you to put others' feelings ahead of your own? Ask yourself why you are doing this. Is it to make them happy? Is it for approval? Is it for love? Is it hope of filling a need for acceptance or worthiness? Is it avoidance of discomfort? Keeping them OK so you can be OK? One of the most powerful questions to continually ask yourself is "Why." Follow the breadcrumbs of each *why* and they will lead you to the root wound. In helping uncover the root, start a journal. Ask yourself, "What is my earliest memory of people-pleasing, sacrificing what I wanted or needed for another's temporary happiness? How did I know it worked? What was my mother, father, grandparent's, or other caretaker's reaction when I was agreeable?"

Is it possible to make your feelings your friends? Is it possible to embrace them, feel them, and let them move through you? We aren't meant to bind to them, we are meant to acknowledge them and allow them to keep moving. Emotions only last ninety seconds (google it!). Their lifespan is short unless we feed them with another thought, which we most often do. I am always surprised how quickly an emotion's actual life span is when I just sit with it and stop running from it. Do the same and see what happens. Acknowledge it. Say, "I am sad," or "I see you, sadness." That emotion may not last as long as you expected.

Our hearts are much like strings on a guitar. If we pay attention, we will notice that in our interactions with others or in events we experience, our heartstrings often get strummed. Sometimes I will notice twinges or sensations in my heart. I don't always notice right away because it is very subtle, and I won't notice if I don't pay attention to my body. When I do notice, I stop what I am doing and say, "Oh! I have been strummed!" Then I will trace back and locate it. You'll know you've found it when you feel the emotional charge or sensation somewhere in your body. Sometimes, it was something I saw on a TV show or something someone said. Acknowledge it and then tell yourself whatever it is you need to hear to relieve the emotion.

Spiritual: The nature of who we truly are is spirit. Deepen your spirituality. This one may be a struggle. We have our own beliefs that usually develop through conditioning from family, culture, society, and religion. What has been *your* experience with God? What is God to *you*? There is no right or wrong answer. Can you allow yourself to explore? If not, ask yourself why not. Would you allow your child permission to explore? Would you allow your child permission to ask questions if they did not understand or felt unsettled about a spiritual concept? You are no less worthy of finding truth in your own way. Find a power greater than you and connect to it as often as you can. Nature is a really great place to start!

When I pleaded with God to show me a way out of my pain, I was led to yoga, a naturopathic doctor, and Glenda—all within two weeks. It doesn't feel coincidental that I was led to practices that would help me in every single layer of my being. I firmly believe their combined forces helped me discover the wholeness I had always longed for. I met my soul on the quiet four corners of my yoga mat. The lens of how I saw myself started to change as I began experiencing *me* in a new way. On my mat, deeply connected to my own breath, I started feeling love, self-acceptance, and peace from the inside out. I didn't know how that was possible. I wasn't *doing* anything to earn it! These experiences reshaped my beliefs about love—maybe it didn't have to be earned, and maybe its true source didn't come from outside of us.

The practice of yoga was the soothing hot wax I had craved for my frayed nerves. Some days, as soon as I hit the mat, tears would flow. I didn't know why or what they were connected to, and it really didn't matter. My body was quickly learning that this was a safe place for me to release, to let go without judgment. After two years of developing my own practice, I became a certified teacher. Yoga changed my life. It was far more than an external practice of postures, it was deeply internal and profoundly spiritual. Tears streamed down my face when

I learned the mantras. I was experiencing the truth of my being, a discovery that went far beyond my physical frame.

Spirituality has been my lifeline. It has changed shape over the course of my life, but it has always been there. Stop listening to your mind and start listening to your heart. Because I trust a higher power, I trust a higher plan and know that everything happens for us: the job you didn't get, the buyer that fell through, the daughter born with a genetic disorder, the stomach cancer you never saw coming. This concept eliminates all victimhood because it didn't happen *to* you, it happened *for* you. Stop trying to humanize God—a force greater than our human minds could ever conceptualize. We ask, "Why would God allow this?" Allow what? Allow us these opportunities to choose love over anything else? I don't know all the ins and outs of God, but I do know that our souls want to evolve and God allows us that chance, however we choose to learn it.

Try this quick guided meditation for connecting with your inner child. Experience in real time how something so simple can hold so much power.

Inner-Child Guided Meditation

Close your eyes and slowly take a deep breath in through your nose. On the exhale, breathe deeply out of the nose. Continuing this cycle, lengthen each breath. Imagine taking your inhale all the way up to the stars, to the one created just for you. Then on the exhale, imagine taking that breath all the way down to the center of the earth, connecting to that one spot meant just for you. Imagine your favorite landscape, a place that feels special to you. It could be the mountains, the ocean, or a beautiful garden. Wherever it is, imagine a bench somewhere in this beautiful, peaceful scene. Keeping your eyes closed, imagine yourself going to sit on the bench. Breathe in the fresh air and find a scent characteristic of this place. Take a few moments to enjoy the beauty and the stillness you feel.

Now imagine your inner child, of a younger age, walking toward you until she's standing directly in front of you. She locks your gaze and you stare deeply into those familiar eyes. You brush her hair out of her face. You take her soft, round cheeks in your hands, look into her eyes, and tell her you love her. Tell her she is not alone; she never has been. Tell her that she is enough, and she doesn't have to try so hard any more to find that validation. Continue by telling her all of the things you needed to hear at that age. Scoop her up, set her on your lap, kiss her little forehead, and gently rock her back and forth as you stroke her hair. Press your warm cheek to hers. And now, thank her. Thank her for all the times she tried to keep you safe the best she could. Thank her for being a survivor, for never giving up. Then tell her she is relieved of the duty she took on. She must be so tired from constantly trying to protect you both. Assure her you've got it now, and you will take care of the both of you. She doesn't have to do it anymore. Give her all the love and nurturing you wanted. Speak the words you wanted and needed to hear.

When you are feeling alone, confused, afraid, and incapable, speak to that little child in you, the one who is hurting. You will be amazed at how quickly you will feel a shift after doing this.

CHAPTER 8

Forgiveness

One day, while sitting in her cozy brown chair, I cried to Glenda. My head hung down with shame. I couldn't even look her in the eye. I felt like such a bad mom. "What if Marley is making tallies against me?" I asked.

"She isn't," Glenda responded. "She isn't capable of it."

My friend Angel wrote this next powerful passage. Tears streamed down my face when I heard her share it for the first time. They were the most tender tears I had ever felt, and they were *for me.*

THE LAW OF INNOCENCE

One of the most common clouds of darkness I encounter personally, and with others, is the practice of attaching to the energies of guilt and shame. Tremendous amounts of pain and suffering can be linked to the attachment to, and perpetual reliving of, guilt and shame associated with our past experiences. Is there any alternative?

Imagine if you and I were in a one-on-one coaching session right now and I looked at you and asked, "Do you know what I am going to ask you next?" You might likely answer the way all of my clients have answered to date: "No."

"Do you know how you're going to answer the next question I ask you, before you know what that question is?" They cannot know what their answer would be. Then I ask, "Are you innocent or guilty at this present moment?" Every time I ask this, clients pause, looking a bit confused, and say, "Innocent?"

Pause and reflect.

How can you be anything other than innocent in the present moment? In any present moment, are you not doing the best you can with all current elements taken into consideration? What if your entire life, often referred to as your "past," is a compilation of one present, innocent moment after another?

Sit with that for a moment. Take a deep breath in. Feel into that.

Notice, as you review your past, in each moment you were doing the very best you could in the circumstances, considering the emotions and the mindset present in each memory. Notice that it is only after the fact that you have looked back on the moments of your life through the lens of fear, shame and judgment. Then, you assigned blame, accountability, guilt, and punishment to yourself and others involved, applying shoulda-coulda-woulda perspectives which were encrypted upon your thinking by external conditioning. And those judgments became part of your story. Each time you revisit a judged memory, you re-experience guilt and shame. But, what might you feel if you recognized the truth—that you were as innocent in each of those past moments as you are in this present moment?

—Angel Lyn, *Soul-U-lar Evolution: A Mormon Woman's Transcendent Journey to Love*

The Spirit of Ubuntu

Ubuntu means "humanity" in some Bantu languages and is often translated as, "I am because we are." I'll share a story the way it was shared with me.

> In a small village, when a woman discovers she is with child, all of her friends and family gather together and go off beyond the borders of the village. There, together, they find the child's song of love that is specific and unique to the unborn child, and under the stars, they sing this child's song of love.
>
> Later, when the woman is nearing delivery, all of her friends and family gather together and again, they all sing this child's song of love as this new life enters the world.
>
> Throughout the child's life—through adolescence and even into adulthood—for birthdays and accomplishments and special occasions, the child is brought to the center of the village. All of the friends and family gather together, encircle the child, and sing their song of love. The child is also brought to the center of the village if they commit a crime or any other offense against the village. Instead of casting out, rejecting, punishing, or isolating the child, all of the friends and family gather around the child and once again sing their same song of love.
>
> What would be the thoughts, feelings, actions, and behaviors of this child, adolescent, or adult moving forward? There is no shame placed on them, no guilt or punishment. In the moment where guilt, shame, rejection, and punishment could be administered, it isn't. Instead, the child is reminded of who they really are. They are flooded with pure love. They are reminded of truth.

There is such a beautiful message in this illustration. Society, family, culture, and religion tell us what a "good mom" looks like, how she speaks, and how she shows love. However you have been showing up as a mother thus far is not wrong, but maybe there are times when greater love could be extended if it starts with self. Mom guilt is all too familiar. We quietly punish ourselves day after day for all the things we *should* be doing. Maybe our pride will not allow us to express those words, let alone offer an apology, but the guilt often plagues us to no end. Maybe we numb that pain with substances—alcohol, pills, food—or mindless TV, or work, chores, laundry, and busyness. You're not alone. What guilt about motherhood do you carry, and what do you do with it?

Can it be that it's time for *you* to be brought to the center of the village? Imagine a circle filled with the people that love you the most gathering around you. Instead of pointing any kind of finger at you, they start singing a song of love to you. It is a song that you already know, and it brings peace to your soul. How do you feel? How do you respond? What does it feel like to be treated with pure, unfiltered, unbiased, unconditional love?

Forgive yourself. Breathe in the forgiveness you feel unworthy to receive. Breathe in compassion for yourself and exhale every bit of guilt, shame, and judgment you have placed on yourself. You are worthy of forgiveness. You are worthy of receiving this kind of love. You have bound yourself in shackles because you feel this is what you deserve. Only you hold the power to unlock your chains, but will you use it?

My first encounter with Angel Lyn was at a retreat I attended in 2022. One evening, right after I shared a portion of my writing from this book, she came and handed me a folded up piece of paper. She encouraged me to read its words aloud. I opened the paper and my eyes welled up with tears. It was my first introduction to the Ho'oponopono prayer.

Mother (parent) Speaking to Herself:

(Say your own name), I am sorry that . . .

(Say your own name), I forgive you for . . .

(Say your own name), thank you for . . .

(Say your own name), I love you!

This is the Hawaiian mediation practice of forgiveness and reconciliation, most commonly used between people. In this situation, I was invited to apply it to myself. Completely on the spot, I allowed this group of women to witness me moving through this process in real time. My statements were raw and unfiltered, with no time for my mind to muddy up what wounds were still present in my heart. Some of the phrases were hard to get out. All of them brought tears. Filling in the blanks with my own words, I read the process aloud to the group:

Karissa, I'm sorry you struggled for so long to change Marley's divine blueprint.

Karissa, I forgive you for all the things you said and did before you knew better.

Karissa, thank you for doing your own healing work so you could show up better for Marley.

Karissa, I love you!

This act of verbalizing regret, forgiveness, gratitude, and love is a powerful step toward healing and mending broken relationships, starting with your own relationship with your self.

"Once a person gives this to themselves, compassion replaces judgment. Then, the person is able to go through the same process for their child." —Angel Lyn in a conversation with me

Marley is so forgiving of me. She always has been. Her soul knows how hard this has been for me and how much I have struggled. Sometimes, I think her higher self is watching me try to navigate this like a flailing fish out of water and thinking, *Girl, you can still swim! You just need to get back in the water!* If she can so easily forgive me and not withhold love from me when I have acted out of my own frustration and pain, then why am I not worthy of giving that gift to myself?

Recently, I was flooded with emotions that leaked out of my eyes. I was feeling so many *sorries* I felt I needed to communicate. *I've already done this,* I thought. Still, though, I ran into the room where Marley was watching TV, draped myself over her, and sobbed a billion sorries. Less than sixty seconds later, Marley patted my head and said, "OK, OK, Mom, that's enough!" I continued on.

"Oh Marley, will you please forgive me?"

"Yes, I forgive you." It was short and simple. I thought it would feel different. I picked myself up and walked out of the room, feeling a little confused, and then it hit me: what I was really asking for wasn't Marley's forgiveness, it was my own.

Pain comes up in layers. Don't let that trip you up when it does. The faster you can give that layer what it's asking for, the faster you can move through it.

I placed my hand on my heart and said, "Karissa, I forgive you. You did the best you could. Forgive yourself."

CHAPTER 9

The Phone Call

We left our faith of origin the year Drey graduated from high school. With that choice, his whole life plan changed too. He didn't know what to do. He walked around the house looking lost and likely feeling a little lost too. That July he chose to move to Texas with a couple of his cousins to sell solar. My heart ***broke!*** I knew this was good for him, but I didn't know how to be complete without him. A part of me held on to him every day. I had entered a new phase of motherhood I didn't know how to do. He left early on a Sunday morning. I'll never forget his face as he turned to leave. He looked terrified and so unsure of himself. I sobbed, and the tears continued every day that week. Every night in my dreams I was with him.

On Thursday morning of the week he left, I had a recurring coaching call. Like so many other times that year, I cried through the whole call. Finally, my coach said to me, "Karissa, can you wrap your son up in light and hand him over to God?"

That thought made me cry even more. It was a struggle at first, and I couldn't do it. A part of me felt like it was my duty to ***not*** let him go, to keep a hole in my heart always open for him, to keep a part of me hurting to show how much I loved him and was still committed to protecting him. I couldn't let go of the feeling that as his mother, I was the only one that could do that. I wrestled back and forth with my feelings, but finally—like bubble wrap—I wrapped him in pure, divine light. Then, I visualized myself scooping him up, just like I did when he was a little boy, and handing him over to God. God received him the same way I gave him over. Drey's divine spirit team surrounded him. I gave over the reins of being his primary caretaker. I turned him over to his team, knowing that they would do an even better job than I could. I felt a knowing that he would be taken care of and supported in a way that was bigger than him. I turned him over to the divine plan he created for himself and allowed it to be . . . partially.

The session ended and I felt so much better. I felt lighter and was comforted knowing Drey was going to be OK in his next phase of life. I was at my friend Rianne's, and we were rehashing the call when my phone rang. It was Marley's school teacher, whom I knew very well. My stomach knotted up as I nervously answered the phone and said, "Jenn, what is it?"

With panic in her voice, she said, "Karissa! Marley just had a seizure at school! The ambulance is on its way! Are you close? Can you come here right now?"

I instantly slingshotted Drey right over to Texas! I realized I hadn't fully given him over because the full investment of trusting in the unknown is *hard!* But this new curve ball with Marley was another level of unknown.

I have never experienced fear the way I did that day. It took hold of me, tightly wrapping its fingers around my throat until I couldn't breathe. Agonizing tears gushed from my eyes, accompanied by an audible wailing cry. I asked Rianne if she could drive me to the school.

I hurried out of her room, quietly asking and praying to God, "What are her agreements? Am I going to lose Marley?" The possibility had never felt so real. As we got to the stairs, I collapsed from such heaviness, my knees buckling underneath me. I sat right there at the top of the stairs and sobbed.

"I can't do this!" I wailed. Rianne scooped me up under my arm and helped me down the stairs. I knew about divine plans and soul agreements. *Is this the agreement? Is this how it ends?* These continued thoughts and questions kept looping as we made our way to the car.

I scrambled for my phone and called Josh. I hardly waited for him to say hello before I blurted out, "Marley had a seizure at school! I'm headed there now! Can you meet me there?" It was quiet on the other end of the phone. I wondered if he even heard me. *Did the bluetooth cut out in his car? Was I going to have to repeat the whole sentence all over again?* With emotions rising I asked, "Are you there? Did you hear me?"

He finally replied, "Yes. This is just one of those phone calls you never want to get." I knew exactly what he meant. His heart dropped too. He said he would meet us at the school.

Marley's classroom was close to a local church that backed up to the school. When we pulled in, a security guard was there waving her hands to guide us in and show us where to go. As soon as the wheels came to a stop, I leapt out of the car and quickly followed another security guard who led me to Marley's classroom. Two more waited just outside her door in the hallway. I paused, hesitating with nerves and fear as I approached the door. I didn't know what I would see or if I was ready to see it. I slowly turned into the classroom and made my way to the group of people huddled around my daughter. I couldn't see her through the desks and all the people.

She was sitting up, crying with her eyes closed. Her color was different from how I remembered it being that morning. She was so pale. She had just regained consciousness when I got there, so she was awake but disoriented. She didn't know where she was or what had happened. I knelt on the floor next to her and tried to put my arm around her with her head resting on my shoulder, as much as she would allow. The EMTs and the paramedics proceeded to update me, but their voices were like white noise in this distorted reality. They asked if I wanted Marley taken to the hospital and if so, which one. I just looked at them, hardly able to process what they were saying. "I don't know," was all I could mumble.

Jenn looked in my eyes and said, "Karissa, you need to take Marley to the hospital. I think you should take her to Mercy Gilbert." That's all I needed: someone I trusted, who was thinking more clearly than I could, to just tell me what to do. I agreed and the paramedics rolled the stretcher into the classroom. They gently lifted Marley's little body up onto it. She'd had a grand mal seizure and urinated through her clothes. I hated the thought of her sitting in those wet clothes.

"Do you want me to get Crew called up front and signed out?" Jenn asked.

Glazed over, I looked at her like a deer in headlights. "I don't know," is all I could get out. Thankfully, she took charge and said she would.

I didn't let myself look at the faces of anyone in the classroom witnessing this scene. I couldn't see their worry or fear—I knew it would just magnify mine. The medics strapped Marley onto the stretcher and carefully wheeled her out of the classroom. Crew walked up as soon as they loaded her into the ambulance. Upon seeing him, I lost it. "Oh, Crewsie!" I threw my arms around him and sobbed! I asked him to go home and grab his sister some clean clothes and meet us at the hospital.

As we parted, Rianne turned to me and asked, "What do you want me to do?"

"Tell everyone!" I said. "We need all of the love and support we can get! Blast it out everywhere!" I gave her a list of people in my contacts and asked her to let them know what was happening. I wanted everyone in my inner circle to know. She sent out mass texts, delivering hard news to the people that loved me and my family the most. She made a personal phone call to my mom. It sounded like she responded in a similar manner I did: she froze and didn't know what to do.

"I really think Karissa needs her mom right now," Rianne told her.

"Really?" she said. "OK!" My mom hurried right over to the hospital. She was only permitted in the waiting room. She texted me when she got there. I pushed through those double doors and as soon as I saw her sitting there, I burst into tears. She got up and met me in a warm embrace and we both sobbed! *What was happening with our little Marley?*

My mom didn't try to fix it or offer solutions. She just listened. She let me cry, and she cried with me. She met me where I was and just let me be there. She showed up in a way I had never experienced her before. It was exactly what I needed.

Over the previous few years, our relationship had changed. We had both changed. When I told her my family was leaving our faith of origin, her reaction completely shocked me: she received me! I have never felt more pure love from her than I did at that time, and it changed everything for me. I saw her differently and I understood her in a way that I couldn't before. So many walls we had each put up to protect our hearts started crumbling as we slowly redefined what our relationship is now.

Crew had arrived at the hospital with a fresh change of clothes before my mom got there. He had to stay in the waiting room because of COVID restrictions. We both burst into tears and met in a tight embrace. I sat by him as we discussed what happened. He said, "I can't help but feel like this is my fault, even though I know it wasn't."

"What do you mean?" I asked.

He said that in between classes, he and a couple of his friends had popped into Marley's classroom to say hi to her. "I saw her sitting on the floor with her friend, playing puzzles. Maybe if I would have stayed a few minutes longer, there is something I could have done to help her."

"Crew, no," I said. "There isn't anything anyone could have done to prevent it! This was not your fault at all!"

It broke my heart that he carried any kind of guilt. I think in his heart he knew it would have happened either way, but his head made him question. Whenever I wasn't by Marley's side in the hospital room, I would completely break down. At one point, a couple came over to me in the waiting room and said, "We don't know what's going on, but we just can't sit here and see you hurting and not offer you love!" I squished them both with grateful tears.

The hospital ran labs and monitored Marley's vitals. Because they didn't really have an explanation, they sent us home, wanting us to follow up with a neurologist. "It could be a fluke," they said. "We really don't have any way of knowing and for a first timer, we don't usually do tests." Before we left the hospital, we made an appointment with a new neurologist.

I wanted to go home but was scared to do so. I was terrified to be responsible for Marley if she had another seizure. I wasn't confident that I knew what to do. Josh and I were given instructions at the hospital, but I don't know how much we really heard or retained.

We got home and got Mar ready for bed. We wanted to keep her close to us, so we made a bed in her favorite spot: on the floor next to Josh's side of the bed. It's where she always wanted to be when she was scared during storms. I asked Josh to trade me places. I wanted to be as close to her as I could. It stormed and rained that night, and Marley crawled up in the bed. Our little dog, Minnie, was right up in there, too, head on my pillow, dog breath right in my face. I didn't even care. I was so happy we were all there together. Marley's warm body breathing right next to me was the most peaceful sound in the world.

The next day I was a mess. I never changed out of my pajamas, and I sobbed all day. The previous day's experience was so traumatic, and we didn't even personally witness the seizure. Presley and Crew chose to stay home from school that day. Crew said he didn't want anyone to ask him how Marley was doing. Even though people meant well, he didn't want to talk about it yet. We all lay on the couch together. Crew and I just wanted to hug and love Mar, sleep next to her, and snuggle her forever. We were so grateful she was home and OK. Most of the time she doesn't like snuggles and pushes us away. "Don't touch me!" she often hollars. We know it's not personal, but it's still hard because that's how we show love. She wants and likes space, but space is the last thing we wanted to give her.

Feeling exhausted, we all hoped Marley would want to lie around and watch a movie with us so we could keep an easy eye on her. She wasn't having that at all! She wanted to play outside. I frantically chased her around with the bottle of rescue meds every time she moved from one place to another. I was so afraid that she would have another seizure. Where would she be or what she would be doing? Would I know what to do? Would she be running down the street and hit her head on the pavement? I was wracked with fear. I didn't want her out of my sight!

I asked Josh if he could take her for a ride-along at some point that day. These rides give me such peace of mind knowing where she is and that she is safe. He came and picked her up that afternoon to give us a little relief. I finally let myself unclench until I realized Josh left the rescue meds! I sat straight up and saw the bottle of pills sitting right on the counter. I had a stage ten melt down! I called Josh straightaway, talk-crying a mile a minute. I was startled to hear Marley say, "Mom, calm down." I didn't realize I was on speaker. It did give me a little laugh. He turned right around to come get the pills.

Fear consumed me as I replayed the day at her school over and over again. When I wasn't replaying that day, I was worrying about "tomorrow." I could not be in the present. I broke down any time someone came over to visit, any time I got a kind message, and any time I was alone. I broke down thinking about the kids in her class that witnessed this scary scene and were concerned for their friend. I broke down thinking about her teachers and how traumatizing it was for them too.

I went to visit Marley's teacher a couple of days later. I had been so concerned for her. Jenn was not just Marley's teacher. We had been in the same church congregation for over fifteen years. We have so much history, and she has known Marley since she was born. Jenn has long-standing sentimental ties to Mar. She said, "As I was performing chest compressions on her, looking into her lifeless blue face, not breathing, all I could see was your face, knowing how much this was going to hurt you! Never in a million years did I ever expect this for Marley!"

I hugged her tightly as I got up to go. I thanked her while feeling deep sorrow for what she had to witness. Walking to my car I pleaded, "Please God, don't make me witness my daughter that way!"

CHAPTER 10

The Dance

I knew I was living in a trauma response. Days later, I felt strong enough to go to those places and work through my feelings. I met with a trusted facilitator to help me move through things. In the process, I remembered the Taoist philosophy of flow: The universe has a natural rhythm, order, and balance. Flow state is moving with it not against it—a non-resistance practice of *going with the flow.* Reaching this place within one's self requires a beautiful dance of surrender and trust.

Through my tears I told the facilitator:

> I have just learned this dance of surrender and trust in mothering Marley. It's like choreography that took me ten years to learn. It was *so* hard! I couldn't get the steps for so long but then finally, I did and was so proud of myself! It took me a decade to surrender my plan for my daughter's path and accept and trust in a higher plan. But what's happening now is completely new choreography, and I don't know how to do this new dance! Marley's spirit wants to be free. She thrives on having the space and freedom to explore, but now the game has changed. The seizure changed everything. I can't let her have

the freedom and space she once did, but I also can't chase her around every day with the bottle of rescue pills! I don't know how to do this!

Something started shifting within me. I felt my mind and body unwind and a softening override my fear. I felt grounded in my body and knew that, somehow, everything was going to be OK. I felt peace, even though I didn't have all the answers. Then, almost instantly, something came through. I was shown that the choreography is actually *the same!* The dance of surrender and trust hadn't changed. The only thing that changed was the music. The steps were the same! *Somewhere inside of you, Karissa, you still know the steps.* That day, I reached new heights in mothering Marley: learning another level of holding on to her while still letting her fly free.

Surrender is not a *giving up*, it is a giving *over*. In this session, I had to give Marley over, *again*. I thought I already had—and I did—but somewhere along the way, I must have taken her back as *mine*. It was an illusion to think I had control or full possession to begin with. She wasn't mine. I am her trusted caregiver. Her soul made agreements before she came here, and I knew I needed to honor them. The more our journey unfolds with Marley, the harder the agreements have been for me to accept. I have to trust that there is a higher purpose in all of it. I have to trust that God has a bigger picture than I do. I visualized scooping her up with my hands and giving her over to God, just like I had days prior with Drey. But this time, I gave everything I wanted for her over, and replaced it with full trust in a higher plan.

By Monday morning (three days after her seizure), Mar was ready to go back to school. I can't say that I was ready to send her. I had to remind myself that I couldn't keep her home forever and that ten eyes on her were better than just the two of mine! *There are good people in place that know what to do. Surrender and trust,* I kept telling myself. *The music is different, but the steps are the same.*

At our first appointment with the neurologist, I was very guarded. She looked at Marley's fourteen-year history and went over notes regarding tests completed as well as the tests we had been advised to do but didn't. "Why didn't you do them?" she asked.

Yikes. I was surprised at how direct she was. "Well," I said, "they seemed super extensive and invasive. We didn't think she needed them." I took a breath, cleared my throat, and swallowed my pride. "But all of that has changed now."

We discussed anti-seizure meds—the pros and cons. We discussed my disapproval of the medication we had used years prior for the absence seizures. The neurologist said some parents like to start meds without knowing the cause of the seizure to spare them from future trauma for themselves and their child. The doctor listened and validated my feelings. I liked her and decided it felt safe to plant roots with her.

I promised myself that I would no longer make choices out of fear. I have done that my whole life. I can still make scary, difficult decisions but out of love and trust. If we did decide to put Marley on new medication, I wanted to feel at peace about it and feel confident that it was the best choice for Marley. I told the doctor that I would have to really feel into it before I made my choice. She said she understood and told me that if I changed my mind, I could call in and they would send in a prescription for her.

Josh's youngest brother overdosed and passed away at thirty years old. He was the life of every party. He was kind, observant, and helpful. For years, we didn't know the extent of his addiction because of how high functioning he was. He had a beaming smile and always gave a tight, warm hug. He addressed by name whoever served him in stores or at restaurants. He never held back a compliment. He made people feel seen. His energy was infectious in the very best way. Behind all of that, though, he was hurting. I wish I'd had the guts then to open the door and talk with him about his hidden pain. Instead, I did what most did and pretended like it wasn't there. I feel closer to Cam now, even though he is no longer here to give warms hugs and kind words. I feel his energy often. When he first passed, I would often dream about him, and the messages in my dreams were so beautiful and comforting to me.

With the drastic change in Marley's circumstances, I was in deep contemplation and continual prayer about it. I wondered how I was going to have a constant eye on her, fearful of where she'd be or what she'd be doing if she had another seizure. One day while sitting in meditation about this, I had a vision. From inside my house, I saw our front door open and Marley walk through it to head outside. As soon as she crossed the threshold of our house, I saw Cam follow her. He followed her as she explored and wandered our little street. When she turned right or left, so did he. He is her guardian angel, her protector. Where she goes, he goes. I saw back to the day she had the seizure at the school. Cam was there. I could see the energy of his hands merge with the Jenn's, and together they performed chest compressions on Marley's little heart.

I believe Cam helped Jenn do something she did not feel strong enough to do on her own at that moment. I sobbed alone in my space, taking in the gravity of this beautiful imagery that was so much more than imagery to me. I felt the support I had temporarily forgotten about and drew so much comfort from it. I didn't want to do medication. We didn't even know what we were dealing with or what this was. I chose not to do it. I'd explore other options.

Five weeks later, Drey was in town for his birthday. We were all in the family room watching TV when Crew yelled, "Mom! Marley is having a seizure!" I leapt off the couch in a panic. "Start the timer!" I yelled as I ran for the bottle of rescue pills. The moment I feared had come. I went to logic and started a running checklist in my mind. Step one: get her on her side. OK, she was there. Step two: "Start the timer!" I yelled to Crew. He didn't even know what I was talking about. We were so unprepared. The kids didn't know what to do. I barely knew what to do! I quickly explained that we needed to time the seizure, and if she wasn't coming out of it on her own by three minutes, we needed to give her the rescue meds.

Step three: watch and wait. The doctor had warned me that those three minutes would be the scariest of our lives. For most, the body will stop on its own and release its own sedative. I understood that it was better if the body could do it on its own. Josh took the role of kneeling down by her and watching her. That was the job I couldn't do. I was frantic, shaking, and scared, fumbling over the damn casing around the pill. The minutes felt like hours. I heard Josh talking to her in a calm, kind voice, saying, "Come on, Marley. Come on."

I didn't look at any of the kids' faces. I couldn't and I wouldn't look at Marley's little face either. What I was presently witnessing was already more than I could handle. She finally started coming to and Josh told me that she didn't need the meds. I felt a huge release inside my body, and it came out in a gush of tears. I collapsed onto the couch and sobbed. I sobbed because she was OK, conscious, and her sweet little face didn't turn blue. I sobbed because we didn't need to give her chest compressions or call 911. I sobbed because the real-life nightmare did not last longer than it did. But soon, all of my gratitude turned to fear. What I had deeply hoped was a fluke—an unexplainable seizure—was clearly not. The seizures were five weeks and three days apart. This was a pattern. That thought tore me apart. Too many unknowns! We called the neurologist that day and started medication.

CHAPTER 11

The Diagnosis

We revisited genetic testing in hopes of finding a diagnosis. We'd been down this road and it had always resulted in a dead-end. The doctor said it would take a few weeks to get the results back from the saliva test. The epilepsy symptom increased our chances of finding the root diagnosis. The last time we'd met with the genetic counselor, they had tested for about fifty of the most common genetic disorders, things like Turner's syndrome and Down syndrome. All of them had come back negative.

Weeks later I got a phone call from the geneticist. "Where are you? Are you home?"

Uh oh. I walked over to the round kitchen table and pulled out one of the black chairs. She continued, "We found it! We found out what Marley has."

I could not believe it! After fourteen years of not knowing, we finally knew! She said it was a rare genetic disorder called CHD2. It affects chromosome 15, which is all neurological. Symptoms are developmental delays, intellectual disability, autism spectrum disorders, neuropsychiatric conditions, ADHD, low muscle tone, and of course, epilepsy. I had never heard of it. My mind was racing. *What did this mean?* I wanted to know more. She advised me to google with caution and that they would gather more information for me from reliable sources. A follow-up appointment was scheduled for a few weeks later and we would discuss action steps moving forward. Guess what I did as soon as I got off the phone with her? I googled! I read as much as I could find, which was super minimal. There wasn't much out there.

The nurse asked me on the phone that day how I was feeling with this new information. The first feeling was relief—no more searching, asking, wondering. Now we knew. I felt a sense of finality, and yet it didn't feel like new information. Once I had finally let myself go to those places, no longer hiding in denial, I *knew.*

The other feeling was deep sadness. I cried for the young mother in me that went everywhere and did everything trying to fix—to *cure*—her daughter. I cried for Marley. *I'm so sorry Marley. I didn't know. But now we know.*

CHAPTER 12

Acceptance

When Marley was a toddler, we were active in our faith of origin: Mormonism. While constantly searching for miracles, I said to Josh, "Maybe we need to show God we are willing to sacrifice to receive a miracle. What if we each go to the temple every week?" The leaders and prophets in this religion promised that blessings would flow when members regularly attended the temple. And so we did. It was a huge sacrifice for both of us. The nearest temple was thirty minutes away and the kids would need sitters.

The thing that kept us so dedicated and committed to going was ***the fear*** that our deepest desire would not be granted if we stopped. Our driving force was the fear that the only way for our daughter to be "better" was on our shoulders. The miracle we wanted depended on us. We had a desired outcome. It was even more than that though. Speaking for myself, I was attached to one particular outcome, and that one only.

I was bargaining, the classic, "If I do this, then you'll do that." Marley was my mirror. She wasn't cracked and broken, I was. I unknowingly projected my wounds onto her. I believed that everything

I was doing was the greatest act of love from a mother for her child. I was wrong. The greatest act of love from a mother to her child is *acceptance*.

The final stage of the grieving process is acceptance.

"Acceptance, as you might imagine, is where the power lies." — David Kessler quoted in "That Discomfort You're Feeling is Grief" by Scott Berinato (March 23, 2020 on hbr.org)

I believe in the power of healing. I also know there must be acceptance for what is. It can be a challenge to distinguish between the two. Recently, I felt a familiar pain in my stomach. I panicked. I went to the worst-case scenario. I spiraled thinking about another surgery, another wound, another something to heal and recover from. I lumped my past experience into something that wasn't for sure going to happen.

I was shocked that nothing showed up on the CT scan! There was no bulge, no apparent hernia, and the surgeon couldn't feel anything concerning. He really wanted to avoid cutting me. There was so much risk of complication because of my past history. "I will go in if you really want me to, but I really don't want to," he said. I left his office in tears. I felt so stuck. *But this pain is so familiar. I know this pain*, I said to myself. An old story had taken over: it was the fear of missing something because the last time we did, I ended up in emergency surgery. I was stuck in an old fear loop. What was I going to do? As I drove home, my mindset changed. I thought to myself, *Well, if it is just something small and I don't need external help, I will just have to heal it myself! I will ask my angels to show me what to do.*

Marley's circumstance is not the same, and I know it, *now*. I am not here to change her, I am here to accept her. Can I accept all parts of her? Can I accept that I will be responsible for raising a child forever?

Josh and I will never be empty nesters, and while it does seem like a very long time to parent like this, there is nowhere else we would have her be than with us. Josh recently said to her, "Are you going to move out of our house one day like Drey, and leave us?" She replied in a firm I-can't-believe-you'd-ask-such-a-question tone, "No!"

Is it possible to get to a place where our children's "failures" or "shortcomings" are not a reflection of us? Is it possible to get to a place where our children's choices, actions, and behaviors are not a reflection of us, their parents? It is possible to embrace what is and let go of what isn't? The answer is yes, but we have to deep dive into why their words, actions, or even who they are strums or activates something in us. What part of us craves acceptance?

Remember the picture I had in my mind for decades? I dreamt of having a little girl of my own. Her favorite color would be pink. She would take dance lessons and I would dress her up every day. I would pierce her ears and paint her nails. We would be best friends! I pictured myself squishing and snuggling her and stroking her soft hair. We would have long chats about everything and nothing. I would hold her little face in my hands, look right into her eyes, and tell her how much I loved her and how long I had been waiting for her to come.

Marley's favorite color is blue. She doesn't take dance lessons, nor does she want to. She doesn't like her nails painted. She doesn't like to wear earrings; I took those out years ago. She doesn't like to snuggle or even be touched. I feel lucky when she lets me hug her for three seconds; we literally count to three! When I try to stroke her hair, she asks me to stop, or says, "OK Mom, that's enough." Eye contact makes her uncomfortable, so she doesn't let me do that for long either. She's not really much for back-and-forth conversation.

It wasn't until she started dressing herself that I noticed what she was choosing was different from what I had been choosing for her. She doesn't like frills or ruffles. She loves to wear oversized tees and a backward hat. She loves to wear some of my big, chunky rings, and sometimes I have to hide my favorites or I'll never find them again! She has such a cool, quirky style that fits her personality so well. This first daughter of mine is the exact opposite of what I had planned and always ***thought*** I wanted. She is so much more. She is exactly what I didn't know I needed. I honor her by allowing her to dress, walk, talk, and act in a way that is completely authentic to her. Sometimes, she wears a Santa hat in July or an old Halloween costume in March. She always turns heads and makes others smile. Sometimes, she likes to wear her brothers' briefs that are longer than her actual shorts. It works for her. She cracks me up!

I don't know what the next ten, twenty, or thirty years will look like for us and Marley, but it will be OK. It would be a gift to have her in close proximity forever, even if that presents its own challenges. She brings joy, light, and humor wherever she goes. There are still so many hard moments, but I am learning the beautiful practice of alchemy. What once felt like a heavy source of pain now feels like an immense source of joy that I hold so much gratitude for. It took time, lots of time, and practice, but I got here! This poem perfectly illustrates the way so many of us feel in regard to a big change in life plans.

Welcome To Holland

by Emily Perl Kingsley

I am often asked to describe the experience of raising a child with a disability - to try to help people who have not shared that unique experience to understand it, to imagine how it would feel. It's like this . . .

When you're going to have a baby, it's like planning a fabulous vacation trip - to Italy. You buy a bunch of guide books and make your wonderful plans. The Coliseum. The Michelangelo David. The gondolas in Venice. You may learn some handy phrases in Italian. It's all very exciting.

After months of eager anticipation, the day finally arrives. You pack your bags and off you go. Several hours later, the plane lands. The flight attendant comes in and says, "Welcome to Holland."

"Holland?!?" you say. "What do you mean Holland?? I signed up for Italy! I'm supposed to be in Italy. All my life I've dreamed of going to Italy."

But there's been a change in the flight plan. They've landed in Holland and there you must stay.

The important thing is that they haven't taken you to a horrible, disgusting, filthy place, full of pestilence, famine and disease. It's just a different place.

So you must go out and buy new guide books. And you must learn a whole new language. And you will meet a whole new group of people you would never have met.

It's just a different place. It's slower-paced than Italy, less flashy than Italy. But after you've been there for a while and you catch your breath, you look around . . . and you begin to notice that Holland has windmills . . . and Holland has tulips. Holland even has Rembrandts.

But everyone you know is busy coming and going from Italy . . . and they're all bragging about what a wonderful time they had there. And for the rest of your life, you will say "Yes, that's where I was supposed to go. That's what I had planned."

And the pain of that will never, ever, ever, ever go away . . . because the loss of that dream is a very very significant loss.

But . . . if you spend your life mourning the fact that you didn't get to Italy, you may never be free to enjoy the very special, the very lovely things . . . about Holland.

CHAPTER 13

Agreements

Before we incarnate on Earth, our souls choose their path. We design them for our own learning and growth. We make vows and promises to those we love for the evolution of their souls, and for our own. I once saw a vision of this with Marley and me.

> I was called forward, and Marley's essence stepped directly in front of me. It was time to finalize terms. A warm, familiar voice said to me, "Do you agree to be this soul's mother? Do you agree to take on the challenges of raising her human life form, which will be completely foreign to you? This agreement will test everything you think you know about love, understanding, compassion, and acceptance. As a young girl, you will lose your voice, but this soul will help you find it once again." I agreed to these terms.
>
> The same familiar voice turned to Marley's essence and said, "Do you agree to be this soul's daughter? Do you agree to take on a physical body with limitations that will be completely foreign to you? Do you accept the terms of this physical body?

Do you promise to help her remember who she is, so she can remember who you are?" This wise soul said yes with strength, conviction, peace, and a deep inner knowing.

She stood before me, eye to eye. My equal. She softly said to me, "You are going to forget who I really am. You will not always be able to see me the way you do now, but I will help you remember what you once knew." She kissed my forehead, sealing in this veil of not knowing. "But," she said, "a part of me will always remember exactly who you are."

Whether this imagery was literal or to illustrate a concept, it doesn't matter. The message is the purpose, and when I saw this exchange, I understood it deeply. I recognized the higher meaning in it.

The greatest force in the universe next to divine love is free will. It is a universal law. All terms were planned and agreed upon in soul form before we ever integrated into these human bodies. There were times when I thought that my daughter may never get asked to a school dance. She may never date. She may never get married or become a mother. She might live with us forever. And my follow-up thought to all that was, ***that is so sad***!

But why is that sad? Is it because I have determined what a happy life looks like? Have I determined what a fulfilled life looks like—what a "normal" life looks like? Why does it have to look a certain way to be happy, acceptable, and fulfilling?

I have learned that all circumstances, situations, and events are actually neutral. It is the human part of us that attaches a positive or negative charge to them. Marley not being asked to a school dance is neutral. I was the one who charged it with sadness. Marley never getting married or becoming a mother is actually neutral. Again, I charged those with sadness. We create suffering within ourselves when we attach to a particular outcome. It isn't ***the thing*** that causes our suffering, it is our ***response*** to the thing. When I have the internal dialogue about her circumstances or feel grief that her life isn't what I thought it would be, I remind myself that somewhere, somehow, Marley agreed to these terms. In some way, she is OK with it, so I must learn to be OK with it too. The sadness I once inserted was my own.

CLOSING

A Mother's Threadbare Prayer

From one mother to another, I warmly extend you an offering of love. I pray for all of the pieces of your heart you keep tied together with that last worn piece of thread. This must be where the saying "hanging on by a thread" comes from. That thread is not a mirror of your strength. It is not indicative of the *capacity* of your strength. It is a reminder that strength still lives somewhere in you.

I pray that you will allow the events and circumstances of your life to turn you inward. I pray that your angels, guides, and the ancestors who walked before you will surround you. May you feel their power, presence, and unending support. What you are doing is so much bigger than what you can presently see. This qualifies you for divine assistance. I pray for divine love to wrap you up from the inside out. No one can do what you're doing better than you. I pray for your child *and* for the child that still lives in you. It is never too late to heal. Healing is a limitless power, unheld by time or space. You *can* do this.

You *are* qualified. Pull your shoulders back and lift your hanging head because you are a match for your mountain.

The things that could have broken me, did! They broke me wide open! Our children with differences aren't broken. They are the menders of broken things. I would never have imagined I could be in a place like this. Mothering Marley has been the biggest roller coaster of my life. I still cry and get frustrated sometimes, but the depth of my ability to love quickly pulls me out of my humanness. Marley reminds me to not take things so seriously and to find the humor in everything. She reminds me to stay young at heart. She reminds me to relax, stay curious, trust, and keep it simple. I feel softness toward a thing I once felt so much resistance to. I even feel it beautifully wrapped up with a silver bow of gratitude. I have given over my limited understanding to a greater knowing and have found so much acceptance and peace in doing so!

In closing, the final prayers I offer up are:

Marley, teach me how to see like you do. Teach me acceptance the way you know it. Teach me to be unapologetically myself, the way you are. Help me remember all the things you already know.

God, give me strength to accept the things I cannot change, courage for the task that seems bigger than me, and peace in knowing that all of this is happening for me.

Made in United States
Troutdale, OR
01/25/2025

28340921R00094